SOUTH DAKOTA
OUTLAWS &
SCOFFLAWS

Published by South Dakota
Magazine, *a bi-monthly
periodical that explores the
history and culture of our
great prairie state.*

Copyright © 2012
South Dakota Magazine
Bernie Hunhoff, Publisher

Editing and writing by
John Andrews, Roger Holtzmann,
Bernie Hunhoff and Katie Hunhoff

Creative Director
Andrea Maibaum

Cover Art
Designed by Rebecca Johnson
Photo courtesy of Adams Museum and House, Deadwood

Library of Congress Catalogue Number
2012944113

Printed in the United States

ISBN
978-0-9744044-3-1

Published by
South Dakota Magazine
PO Box 175, Yankton, SD 57078
(605) 665-6655
www.SouthDakotaMagazine.com

SOUTH DAKOTA
OUTLAWS &
SCOFFLAWS

*Did Outlaws and Scandalous Ancestors
Shape South Dakota's Culture?*

By John Andrews, Bernie Hunhoff, Roger Holtzmann & Katie Hunhoff

Contents

Introduction: *Why We're Curious About Outlaws*   vii

Chapter 1: *The Yankton Ring*   1

Chapter 2: *Cuthbert DuCharme: The French Dandy*   11

Chapter 3: *The Awful Al Swearengen*   17

Chapter 4: *Agents of the Road*   29

Chapter 5: *Shooting in Saloon No. 10*   39

Chapter 6: *Fallen Angels*   49

Chapter 7: *Hangman's Hill*   59

Chapter 8: *The Unwickedest Outlaw*   67

Chapter 9: *Lame Johnny*   73

Chapter 10: *Miners & Miscreants*   81

Chapter 11: *Poker Alice*   89

Chapter 12: *Jack Sully: The Rosebud's Robin Hood?*   95

Chapter 13: *Entrepreneurs & Opportunists*   105

Chapter 14: *Richard Pettigrew*   113

Chapter 15: *The Death of LeBeau*   123

Chapter 16: *Calamity Jane: The Legend and the Lout*   131

Index   139

Acknowledgments

The word "acknowledgments" is insufficient. We mean to say "thank you!" to all who helped us collect these stories. Gracias. Danke. Gratis. Merci. Xièxie. That won't cover all the languages spoken in Deadwood during the gold rush days that are so prominent in this book. But it's a good start.

Gracias to our fellow *South Dakota Magazine* staffers for proofreading, designing and otherwise supporting us. They include Jana Lane, Andrea Maibaum, Rebecca Johnson, Laura Johnson, Heidi Marsh and Ruth Steil.

Danke to Paul Higbee, a longtime contributor to the magazine who wrote about Poker Alice.

Merci to all the hometown historians who offered advice and directions — among them Jim Lane, Jack Broome, Bob Hanson, Jerry Wilson, Ron Dufek, Pat Morrison and all the others we can't recall at press time.

And many thanks to the distinguished South Dakota organizations who not only made this book possible, but have been wonderful partners in helping us publish *South Dakota Magazine* through the past three decades: the South Dakota State Historical Society, the Journey Museum of Rapid City, the Dakota Territorial Museum in Yankton and the Adams House and Museum in Deadwood.

South Dakota is a diverse and interesting state where the Old West is alive and flourishing. We thank our 810,000 fellow South Dakotans for keeping it that way.

INTRODUCTION

Why We Care About Outlaws

You ask about my conscience
And I offer you my soul
You ask if I'll grow to be a wise man
Well I ask if I'll grow old.
— Bon Jovi, "Blaze of Glory"

AMERICANS' FASCINATION WITH Old West scofflaws and scoundrels never seems to fade. That says something about who we are in the 21st century — a nation of sentimentalists who love adventure, root for underdogs, and somehow reconcile the difference between the virtues we claim to admire and the rogues we find so interesting. We nod in agreement on Sunday morning when our minister preaches the Ten Commandments, yet every one of them was broken countless times in Deadwood, Yankton and many places in between by the romanticized rogues you are about to meet in this book.

Songs have been sung of them, and movies made. Their misdeeds have shaped history. Our culture is rife with stories of horse thieves, con artists, snake oil salesmen and worse.

Generally, we soften the images of our outlaw ancestors. Al Swearengen was a pimp and a woman-beater but the HBO series *Deadwood* showed him as a brothel owner and town builder with a soft side. Doris Day portrayed Calamity Jane as a blonde beauty in fashionable buckskin who could ride, shoot and sing like a mountain goddess. Elizabeth Taylor played Poker Alice for a greatly fictionalized 1987 movie in which the gorgeous gambler unknowingly buys a brothel.

Hollywood script writers aren't the only ones who rewrite history to suit themselves. My favorite whitewash appeared in a family genealogy I read years ago. As memory serves, it went something like this: "Our grandfather sadly passed away shortly after giving a speech in the public square. He was on his horse at the time and he fell from the horse just after speaking and broke his neck." There was no mention of the fact that grandpa's neck happened to be attached to a rope that was attached to a tree.

Every corner of the United States has its favorite outlaws and villains, but few places have the rogue-rich history of Dakota Territory and South Dakota. Maybe that's because this last frontier was so quickly transformed from a nomadic Native American culture to a robust conglomeration of cowboys, Indians, traders, miners, ranchers, immigrants, soldiers, farmers, railroaders and entrepreneurs.

Seldom in U.S. history have so many diverse people come together in such a short time to create a civilization. Those who came, whether from Nebraska or Norway or points in between, were the most adventurous or the most desperate sorts. Sometimes both. The faint of heart didn't leave family, friends and the comforts of home for the uncertainties and dangers of life on the frontier. Dakota Territory attracted big dreamers, the bold and brave hungering for a fresh start. Immigrant farmers who couldn't find 40 acres to plow in Norway or Germany. Civil War veterans who couldn't find peace in Pennsylvania or Illinois after surviving the bitter war in the South. Poor men, unlucky men, greedy men who were tempted by stories of gold lying about on the ground, or opportunists eager to capitalize on the gold-diggers.

Cowboys followed cattle from Texas and Oklahoma. Chinese came to work the mines and build railroads. Many of the gamblers dug for gold or played the poker tables, but other risk-takers bought lots in the dozens of towns that were staked out, 10 miles apart, like garden plots along the train tracks.

Some of our Wild West cities have already disappeared, and others are now counted as ghost towns. Still, South Dakota is a babe when it comes to the world's civilizations. Romans will forever study Caesar, Nero and Plato. New Englanders remember the Puritans, Pilgrims and whalers. Here in Dakota Territory, our folk stories are of brave adventurers, soft-hearted heroes and villains, some of whom were all the above.

Awhile back, we wrote about some favorite scoundrels in *South Dakota Magazine.* We told the story of a would-be miner who bought claims along Box Elder Creek in the Black Hills. He allegedly spread rumors that his mine contained more gold than the Homestake Mine at Lead, which was quite a success by then.

Newspapers in Chicago reported the find, which enabled the enterprising fellow to attract some investors and a partner who was a mineralogist to boot. Some say they salted the mine to sweeten the deal. Investors suspected they were being suckered when the mineworkers processed 3,000 tons of ore and only extracted $5 worth of gold. The two partners blamed each other for the swindle and they parted ways. It's a good story, unless the entrepreneurial miners were your ancestors. As soon as our magazine hit the streets, we got a call from a West River lady who lamented, "My grandfather was not a crook!" Apparently, the fellow did raise a nice family and contributed in positive ways to early-day South Dakota.

Here in our hometown of Yankton, local citizens are sometimes surprised when they learn that the city's founders — Picotte and Burleigh, for example, who have streets named after them — were carpet-bagging swindlers.

One man's crook might be another man's grandpa, or another town's favorite son. Jack Sully, the Robin Hood of the Rosebud country, has countless descendants scattered across South Dakota, including a Catholic nun. But the Sully cousins seem quite proud of Grandpa Jack's exploits. We've written about his crimes and punishments many times with nary a complaint from the family.

Truthfully, any man or woman's life is a mosaic of a thousand actions, so we shouldn't judge an individual by any single happening — unless he murders Wild Bill Hickok in a saloon or beats the women in his brothel. Some of our outlaws and scofflaws are beyond defense, but most were complex adventure-seekers living in complicated times.

We live among reminders of that frontier society. The West River grasslands, mountains and wild rivers are largely unchanged. You can still sip beer in Saloon No. 10, where Wild Bill was shot. Ruts of stagecoach routes remain visible in the short grass country, and trees used for hangings still sprout leaves in the spring.

The main writers of this book (myself, John Andrews, Katie Hunhoff and Roger Holtzmann) are among a small staff that publishes *South Dakota Magazine* from a set of buildings constructed in old Yankton by Territorial Governor John Pennington in the 1870s. He was governor when the Black Hills was opened to mining, when Custer was killed at the Little Big Horn, and when McCall was hanged on the city's north side.

Pennington was part of the Yankton gang that profited from their brief control over Dakota Territory. He created Pennington County, for example, then named his Yankton cronies to serve as county officials. Most of them took the salaries but named deputies to do the work in the Black Hills. Even so, Pennington is considered more honest than many of the territorial officials; he sided with farmers over the railroads, and he showed concerns about the treatment of Native Americans.

South Dakota remains the center of the American frontier. We can't escape our past so we may as well embrace the good, the bad and the ugly that is our heritage. One clear truth that emerges is this: our Dakota frontier attracted every kind of man and woman that you can imagine, the virtuous and the opportunist, the brave and the weak, the outsider and the operator. Frontiers do that.

We are a gang of conformists today, at least in comparison to the characters you'll read about in this book. But you've opened the cover and read this far. That's an indication you may have a genetic strain of the immigrant farmer, the gold-digger, the poker player and itinerant cowboy. Or maybe you just enjoy reading about the frontier, and about the people who came here before us.

Hopefully you won't find any reference to your grandfather or grandmother, but if you do please know this was written without malice or mischief.

Bernie Hunhoff, editor & publisher
South Dakota Magazine

Outlaws & Scofflaws

CHAPTER 1

The Yankton Ring

WHEN DAKOTA TERRITORY came into being on March 2, 1861, the new settlers were clustered in the extreme southeastern corner, in Sioux Falls and a handful of settlements along the Missouri River. One of those upstart towns would win the much coveted prize of territorial capital. Yankton was a dark horse at the start, running behind Sioux Falls and Vermillion, but its leaders had an ace up their communal sleeve.

John B.S. Todd had come to the region in 1855 as an Army officer stationed at Fort Randall, but he soon quit the military to start a trading company. In the course of doing business, Todd made many contacts with Indians along the river, and he was instrumental in arranging the first land cession by the Yankton tribe. When the treaty was finalized he and his partners were rewarded with choice land grants, including several in what became the city of Yankton. Those grants, needless to say, would gain value if Yankton was the capital.

As luck would have it, John Todd knew someone who was in a position to influence the decision: his cousin, Mary (Todd) Lincoln. "Historian Doane Robinson credited Mrs. Lincoln's intercession as the deciding factor in ... Yankton's selection as the seat of government," wrote Bob Karolevitz in *Yankton: A Pioneer Past.*

Todd wanted to be the territory's first governor, but that honor went instead to William Jayne, a Lincoln family friend from Illinois. Jayne arrived in Sioux City in May of 1861, and as he made his way to Yankton the citizens of Vermillion lavishly entertained him. They were miffed when it later became apparent that the capital's location had already been determined: their party was a waste of money.

There was a messy fight when the first territorial legislature met to confirm the decision — at one point a group of Yankton supporters threatened Speaker George M. Pinney's life, or at least his health — and the matter wasn't settled until some old-fashioned horse trading had taken place. Vermillion was promised a university, Bon Homme a prison, and Yankton got the capital. Even so, there was resentment in the jilted communities, and over time grumbling about the "Yankton Ring's" dominance of territorial politics only got worse.

With the capital question settled, the next step was to elect a territorial delegate to Congress — an important position because the delegate could reward his supporters with federal patronage jobs, and as often as not line his own pockets. As a result, "gross irregularities characterized the early elections [in Dakota Territory]," wrote Herbert Schell. "Bribery, vote buying and illegal voting were openly charged and often proved …. Political factions in an attitude of 'rule or ruin' resorted to every known device to win." Such an atmosphere was tailor-made for Dr. Walter Atwood Burleigh.

Walter Burleigh lined his pockets with money skimmed from provisions meant for Indians in Dakota Territory.

Burleigh had helped deliver the state of Pennsylvania to Abraham Lincoln in the election of 1860, and the good doctor wasn't shy about cashing in on his service. He suggested the president show appreciation by appointing him ambassador to Great Britain. Lincoln countered with an offer to be the Indian agent for the Yankton Sioux, in the decidedly less refined Dakota Territory.

The doctor hid his chagrin by pointing out that an Indian agent's salary would be insufficient to provide his family with their accustomed level of comfort. "I would be forced to either steal or starve," he said with all the dignity he could muster.

"Dr. Burleigh," Lincoln replied, "if I am any judge of character, you will not starve."

Honest Abe never spoke truer words. There was a saying on the frontier that if a man became an Indian agent he could steal himself rich. Agents routinely confiscated annuity goods meant for the Indians and resold them; they rewarded supporters with contracts to supply beef to the reservations, then looked the other way when sickly cattle and putrid meat were delivered; funds intended for the tribes disappeared in a fog of dubious accounting.

Burleigh was a man of unquestioned ability and a tireless promoter of the territory; he was also, "as unscrupulous an Indian official or politician as ever set foot on Dakota soil," wrote Harry Anderson in *Fur Traders as Fathers*. Burleigh exploited every larcenous scheme known to Indian agents during his tenure and expanded the possibilities for plunder by making fraud a family enterprise. He appointed his father-in-law, Andrew Faulk, as the Yankton Agency's chief clerk, kept his daughter on the payroll as a teacher, even though there was no school on the reservation, and paid his 13-year-old son $80 a month as a clerk.

With the Yankton Agency as a source of cash and influence, Burleigh set his sights on becoming the Congressional Delegate for Dakota Territory. He easily won office in 1864, but his unparalleled thievery had by then drawn the attention of a Congressional committee. They visited the Yankton reservation in 1865 and heard enough to recommend an inquiry by the Indian Bureau. Their investigator came away, "so impressed with the payroll padding, graft and nepotism practiced by the able, jovial doctor ... that his report was written in a tone that sounded less like condemnation than respectful awe," wrote Howard Lamar, an esteemed Dakota Territory scholar.

Burleigh shifted the blame for his troubles onto the second Territorial Governor, Newton Edmunds, who had cooperated with the Congressional committee. Unfortunately for the governor, fate soon presented the master manipulator Burleigh with an opportunity to make him pay.

Andrew Johnson succeeded the assassinated Lincoln as president in 1865, which worked out well for Burleigh, his political ally. Burleigh charged Edmunds with stealing money from the Indian Bureau, of all things, and urged President Johnson to remove the governor from office. Johnson and the Edmunds clan were at odds over unrelated issues at the time, so the president was more than happy to oblige. For the *coup de grace*, Burleigh got Faulk appointed as Edmunds' replacement.

Burleigh was re-elected as delegate in 1866 despite his legal troubles. Faulk took office that same year, which put all the territorial levers of power at the doctor's command. This marked the zenith of Burleigh's political career, and with his newfound clout he was able to make his Indian Bureau troubles go away.

Faulk lost the governorship when Ulysses S. Grant became president, and Burleigh was defeated in the election of 1868. There would be no respite for the territory, however, because their regimen of greed and shady dealing was ably carried forward by Faulk's replacement, John A. Burbank.

Burbank arrived in his mud street capital at a time of rancorous political troubles, but there was a twist. Divisions within the Republican ranks were at least as bitter as those between the Democrats and Republicans. Burbank's presence made this problem worse because he viewed the governorship as a business opportunity and little more; public affairs were important only so far as they affected his economic interests.

Railroads were on every dreamer's and schemer's mind during this era, and Governor Burbank was no exception. He greased the wheels for Yankton's investment in the Dakota

Southern Railway Company, which brought rails to town in 1873, and he was rewarded with a seat on the line's board of directors. Burbank then turned and lobbied Congress to get the line extended to Springfield — where he coincidentally held substantial business interests.

For many investors, getting tracks laid and running a railroad were secondary matters. Financial manipulations were seen as the way to make real money. Burbank and the other Dakota Southern directors hatched such a scheme in 1873 when they proposed to have the company issue $1.2 million worth of additional bonds. This would have seriously watered down Yankton County's ownership stake in the company, so the county commissioners obtained an injunction against the sale from Judge A.H. Barnes. Governor Burbank responded by threatening to banish Judge Barnes to the Pembina judicial district, hundreds of miles north on the Canadian border.

Yankton's movers and shakers backed either Burbank and the directors or the county commissioners, and the feud escalated to a point where cooler heads thought it advisable to call a public meeting to clear the air. Just the opposite happened, of course.

Banker Peter Wintermute and Territorial Secretary Edwin S. McCook were on opposite sides of the issue, with McCook being an outspoken Burbank supporter. There was bad blood between them before that night, so it's a mystery why Wintermute chose to ask McCook for a cigar. McCook rudely refused, and for good measure the burly secretary thrashed the diminutive banker, even pushed his face into a spittoon. Wintermute retired from the meeting to clean up, then returned with a revolver and fatally wounded McCook, who died on September 12, 1873.

Edwin McCook's murder shocked the factions into attempting to reconcile, but outside events soon made the Dakota Southern's bond issue moot. A Northern Pacific Railroad financing scheme hatched by Jay Cooke & Company imploded, which caused the bank to fail and initiated a daisy chain of bank failures across the country. The Panic of 1873, as this sequence of events came to be known, plunged the nation into a depression and dried up the market for bonds of any kind.

In the wake of all this, one thing united the residents of Dakota: most of them wanted to be rid of John Burbank. They circulated petitions against the governor and gathered 1,200 signatures. Burbank spent more time in Washington and at his home in Indiana than in Dakota during his term so being personally unpopular didn't matter much, but given the times there weren't any business opportunities left in the territory. He resigned, tallied up his profits and moved on to greener pastures.

John L. Pennington was appointed in Burbank's stead. His contribution to Yankton's reputation for high-handedness came after the territorial legislature established three new counties, Custer, Lawrence and Pennington, in the Black Hills. The law authorized Governor Pennington to appoint officials for the new counties, and he unwisely filled the positions with his Yankton cronies rather than locals. That caused an understandable uproar, which only got worse when the new officials didn't even bother to move west. Pennington then compounded his blunder by selecting Sheridan over Rapid City as the county seat of his namesake county. Rumors abounded that Pennington and the Yankton Ring had a financial stake in the new town site, fueling resentment against the "corn growers" who ran the territory. There was even talk of severing the Black Hills from Dakota and attaching the region to Wyoming.

Locally elected officials soon replaced Pennington's appointed ones, but the governor's unpopularity in the Black Hills persisted. He was succeeded by William A. Howard in 1878. Howard was a decent, conscientious man, but by the time he took office he was also "old as well as ailing," according to Herbert Schell. Howard relied heavily on the Yankton Ring for advice, with predictable results.

The ring then included Burleigh and Faulk, along with numerous other former office holders who still lived in Yankton.

They knew how to manipulate the system, especially in the territorial legislature, which moved one disgruntled editor to characterize that body as "a howling mob of gangsters and corruptionists ... led by the nose by one or two tricksters whose whole object is to fill their pockets by schemes of jobbery and plunder."

Fortunately for all who despised the Yankton Ring's hold on the territory, delivery was at hand. William Howard died on April 10, 1880, and Nehemiah G. Ordway was appointed to replace him. Tall and stern, Ordway looked every inch a statesman, and his haughty manner was that of a schoolmaster come to set the unruly children of Dakota straight. In his first message to the legislature he made it clear that he saw his first duty as preparing the territory for statehood. Most people were in favor of statehood so that was well-received. Unfortunately for the vested interests, Ordway believed that process required him to reform a number of "radical defects" in the territory's legal structure and change the way some things had always been done.

Ordway and the Yankton Ring initially found common cause against the supporters of Richard Pettigrew, the territorial delegate and Ordway's political rival. By 1883, however, Ordway's personal arrogance and dictatorial methods had soured the relationship. This was unfortunate timing for Yankton because they were about to need every friend they could get.

Andrew Faulk looked after his family and friends when he was appointed governor of Dakota Territory in 1866.

Governor Ordway's time in office coincided with the beginning of the Dakota Boom. As more and more people arrived during the 1880s the territory's center of gravity began to shift. Yankton's residents conceded that the capital would one day have to be removed to a more central location, but they hoped to delay that move at least until the territory became a state. This was not to be.

The issue of whether and where to relocate the capital dominated the legislative session of 1883. Ordway made his sympathies clear by approving legislation introduced by those who favored relocation, and vetoing measures put forward by those who argued against the move. Government jobs were parceled out. Legislators from Brookings and Fargo won support for projects at their respective universities. Outright bribes of $5,000 were paid for individual votes, at least according to the Yankton Ring. After all the logrolling and infighting, a nine-man commission was created to choose the capital's new location.

Those who opposed the capital's relocation got an injunction to prevent the commission from organizing in Yankton, as required by law, but for once the Yanktonians were outmaneuvered. The commission's members met secretly in Sioux

Governor Nehemiah Ordway earned the scorn of Yanktonians when he presided over the effort to relocate the territorial capital to Bismarck in 1883.

City, then boarded a special train consisting of an engine and one car. They reached the city limits of Yankton at six in the morning on April 3, 1883, and while the city slept they duly organized themselves according to the letter of the law. "Quickly thereafter the locomotive towed its cargo of connivers out of town on a junket to inspect the communities competing for the governmental plum," wrote Karolevitz.

Like Yankton at the beginning of the territorial era, Bismarck was considered a long shot in the capital contest. They finally prevailed on the

Andrea Maibaum

CAPITOL IN THE PARK

A plaque at the corner of Fourth and Capital in downtown Yankton marks the site of the original territorial capital building. Though it was demolished decades ago, artifacts from our first capital building are preserved at the Dakota Territorial Museum. They include a wall clock, seal stamper, ledger, a gavel made from wood used in the building, a double desk from the trial of Jack McCall and the capital's original black walnut door.

Today a replica of the capital stands in Riverside Park. It is open daily during the summer, and National Park Service staff offers interpretive programs inside and nearby at the double-decker Meridian Bridge, now a pedestrian walkway and bicycle path.

A major street on the east side of Yankton bears Burleigh's name, and he and many of his cronies are buried in the historic Yankton Cemetery on the north edge of town.

commission's 13th ballot, a victory made possible in part because the more numerous southern delegates could never agree on a common candidate.

Yankton's residents were furious over the move and they fixed on Ordway as the villain. They accused him of conspiring with Alexander MacKenzie, a commission member and Northern Pacific Railroad lobbyist who reportedly sold more than $250,000 worth of Bismarck real estate shortly after the capital decision. Whether Ordway did or not is unclear. Either way, he shed no tears over the result, and Yankton's stranglehold on Dakota Territory — borne of favoritism, nurtured by political maneuvering and corruption — quietly came to an unlamented end.

CHAPTER 2

Cuthbert DuCharme
French Dandy with a Temper

LEGEND SAYS $50,000 in gold is buried somewhere in the Missouri River valley west of Geddes, but it will take a strong swimmer with a shovel to find it.

It's supposedly the lost treasure of Cuthbert DuCharme, a roughhousing fur trader who ran a trading post and roadhouse along the river for nearly 30 years. DuCharme is one of the most colorful rogues in South Dakota's fur trade history. He was charitable with downtrodden local families, but it's also believed he was capable of heinous murder.

Cuthbert DuCharme was born in Sault Ste. Marie, Ontario, Canada in 1827. His ancestors were prominent fur traders who had lived around the Great Lakes, Ontario and Quebec since the early 18th century. DuCharme worked for the American Fur Company, which sent a delegation of traders to establish posts in the Upper Missouri River valley in the 1850s and 1860s. He was one of the earliest pioneers to settle in present day Charles Mix County when he arrived in 1857. He claimed 260 acres of pristine river valley land near a freshwater spring two miles east of Wheeler and built a trading post.

Fur trading was big business in the Missouri River valley in the 19th century. The Missouri Fur Company, the North West Company, Hudson's Bay Company and the American Fur Company all had a presence in the Upper Missouri, defined as the portion of the Missouri River above the mouth of the Big

Sioux. People like John Jacob Astor and Pierre Chouteau grew rich off Great Plains wildlife. Beaver pelts were prized possessions in the early 19th century, but in the 1850s and 1860s 100,000 buffalo robes were shipped annually to St. Louis to satisfy the market. Fashion trends in urban America and Europe largely determined whether trappers caught mink, coyote, deer, beaver, buffalo, otter, raccoon or some other varmint.

As many as 100 trading posts stood in present day South Dakota, mostly along the Missouri River. The large and well fortified Fort Pierre was an intimidating structure, but others, as Rex Myers wrote in *A New South Dakota History*, were "often just crude cabins used to gather furs for trans-shipment or as winter residences for free trappers."

DuCharme's 30-by-40-foot post was constructed from tall, river valley cottonwoods. The main floor included a round wooden table and four chairs where DuCharme's clientele — traders, cowboys, steamboat hands, drifters and soldiers from nearby Fort Randall — played poker and drank whiskey from a huge vat with three cups chained to it. A quarter bought a cupful (about a half pint) of booze. DuCharme quickly gained a reputation for his whiskey and earned the nickname "Old Papineau," translated as *pap water*, or whiskey.

Legend says Cuthbert DuCharme, an early fur trader who ran a roadhouse along the Missouri River, buried $50,000 in gold coins somewhere in the Charles Mix County river valley.

Julius Luse, a soldier stationed at Fort Randall, described DuCharme as "a man of fine physique, exquisite as a French dandy and a most gracious host, but when intoxicated a veritable devil." DuCharme's drunkenness led to violent encounters with his wife Theresa, whom he married in 1862, and their six children. Luse recalled spending an evening at the home of DuCharme's neighbor. One of Old Paps' sons had sought refuge there after running afoul of his father, who had threatened to shoot him. Later that night, the soldiers returned to DuCharme's post, where they were spending the night. At bedtime they heard a scuffle. They peered through floorboard cracks and found DuCharme, grasping his wife's hair and spinning her so violently that part of her scalp was ripped from her head. The soldiers returned to the neighbor's house, with DuCharme following. When he arrived and leveled his gun, the soldiers jumped and disarmed him. "His hands were bound and he was trussed by running the gun barrel under his knees and over his bound arms, and he was rolled into a corner to simmer down and sober up," wrote Charles Mix County historian Stanley Votruba.

But he could be just as violent when sober. On a trip to Yankton, DuCharme left Henry Bradley's livery barn without paying. When Bradley protested, DuCharme raised an Army needle gun, pointed it at Bradley and pulled the trigger. The gun misfired, and Bradley used the small window of opportunity to knock DuCharme out with a club. But when police arrived, it was Bradley they arrested and sent to jail.

On another of his regular trips to Yankton to purchase whiskey, Judge Ellison Smith asked if he could ride with DuCharme as far as Springfield. As DuCharme's pair of stallions led them down the Bon Homme Road, DuCharme asked his guest if he wanted to try a French ride. Smith, not knowing what Old Paps intended, expressed interest. DuCharme tossed the reins aside, grabbed a heavy whip and lashed his horses into a furious sprint. They ran until they were exhausted. Judge Smith was shaken, but uninjured.

At times DuCharme and his cronies were the only law in his area of Charles Mix County. The federal government, trying to rid the region of unauthorized whiskey houses, continually moved the strip of land containing Papineau's post between the Yankton Indian Reservation, the Fort Randall Military Reservation and the public domain. Squatters who settled in what became known as Papineau Flats responded by creating their own form of government that did nothing but ensure, through bribery and intimidation, that the right men were elected to office. When Charles Mix County was formally organized in 1862, Papineau's trading post became Papinaville, and was named county seat, a distinction it held until 1869.

DuCharme's post did brisk business. A well-traveled military road used by Gen. Alfred Sully in 1863 and Lt. Col. George Custer in 1873 passed just beyond his door. "Military and government travelers considered the Papineau Flats/Fort Randall locality the wildest and toughest on the river," Votruba wrote. "Drunkenness was common and murder not unusual." A local banker recalled that DuCharme frequently ran advertisements in Chicago newspapers offering cheap land. Respondents, especially women, were lured to his place, robbed, killed and buried in the DuCharme Cemetery, just behind the cabin. Decades later, when Missouri River flooding washed part of the cemetery away, the U.S. Army Corps of Engineers relocated the remains. They found 27 graves, 14 of which were unidentified.

DuCharme was not afraid of gunplay. In 1867, Charles Campbell opened a trading post near the mouth of Campbell Creek, about a half mile from Paps' cabin. If one noticed the other's store seemed busy, they sometimes stood in their doorways and took pot shots at each other. A friend confronted Paps about his violent behavior, cautioning that if it continued he might be shot. DuCharme smugly replied that powder and lead couldn't hurt him. Then he pointed a revolver to his face and shot himself through the mouth. His only injury was a few missing teeth.

DuCharme ran his trading post until 1885, when he and his wife moved west of the Missouri River and settled south of Bonesteel. There they ran a store and led a quieter life, but Old Paps' decades of drinking and carousing eventually caught up with him.

When Theresa DuCharme died in 1900, the legend of Paps'

buried treasure began to form. During his heyday, DuCharme was said to be worth $75,000. As he grew older, he became paranoid about the safety of his fortune and smart enough to know that he might waste it on gambling and booze. Legend says he gave Theresa $50,000 in gold and told her to bury it somewhere near his trading post for their retirement. But she died suddenly and unexpectedly; her horse spooked, a foot caught in the stirrup and she was dragged to her death. No one alive knew the treasure's secret location, and Old Paps spent his last years digging for his lost money. He suffered a mental and physical breakdown and was admitted to the State Hospital in Yankton.

He died there on January 12, 1903. If a fortune is buried

SEE FOR YOURSELF

See Old Paps' cabin at the Geddes Historical Village. Geddes is about 70 miles northwest of Yankton on Highway 50. The cabin stands in a pretty park with other historical buildings, including Governor Peter Norbeck's childhood home, a WNAX gas station, an 1895 schoolhouse used in southern Charles Mix County from 1901 to 1948, a 1900 claim shanty and a replica keelboat built for the Lewis and Clark bicentennial in 2004. For information, call (605) 337-2501.

somewhere along the Missouri, it's likely under 30 feet of water. Lake Francis Case, created by the Fort Randall Dam, flooded Wheeler and the land where Paps' cabin once stood.

DuCharme's trading post remained a private residence until the 1930s, when a farmer bought it to use as a granary. Later, he sold the building to the Geddes Historical Society, which moved the cabin into Geddes in 1972. In 1984, historian Stanley Votruba, who had collected the gravestones from the DuCharme Cemetery, placed them next to Paps' cabin. Today the cabin and stones are centerpieces of the Geddes Historical Village and reminders of a colorful and adventuresome era of South Dakota history.

CHAPTER 3

The Awful Al Swearengen

'Liar, Cheat and Flesh Peddler'

FIRST CAME the tin pan prospectors, men on the run from settled lives who dreamed of finding gold in the Black Hills of Dakota. Hard on their heels was a host of unholy types, from card sharks to prostitutes to gunslingers, who knew that a more certain path to riches was to wait until others had found gold and then relieve them of their burdensome newfound wealth.

Saloons were the natural habitat of both prey and predator. By the middle of 1877 there were more than 70 such establishments in Deadwood. Most were ramshackle, here today, gone tomorrow affairs with only one item on the bill of fare: overpriced whiskey, "whose effect on the uninitiated lasted up to a week and tended to incapacitate the victim for any useful activity whatever," wrote Watson Parker in *Deadwood: The Golden Years*.

Deadwood pioneers also enjoyed a number of surprisingly well-appointed "sporting houses" that brought liquor, prostitutes, theatrical shows and gambling together under one roof. Of these, none was grander or more infamous than the Gem Theater, operated by Al Swearengen.

Swearengen, "was a liar, a cheat, a flesh peddler and a spendthrift," according to Erik Iverson, who researched Swearengen's life for his master's thesis. Those might be considered unremarkable, even desirable attributes for a saloon keeper,

Al Swearengen's Gem Theater hosted professional theater and fallen angels. Swearengen is thought to be the third man from the right.

Photo courtesy of the Adams Museum, Deadwood

but Swearengen managed to distinguish himself even in that infamous fraternity.

Ellis Albert Swearengen was born of modest pioneer stock in Oskaloosa, Iowa Territory, in 1845. Daniel and Keziah Swearengen packed up and headed west when news of gold strikes in California reached them, but after two fruitless years they returned to Oskaloosa and Daniel opened a butcher shop. When Ellis and his twin brother Lemuel came of age during and after the Civil War, Lemuel was taken into the family business as a meat cutter's apprentice. Daniel supplied Ellis with

the capital to purchase a team and wagon to start a delivery service.

Al, as he now preferred to be called, kept his hack "busy from sun-up to sun-down," wrote Iverson. "If money could be made, Swearengen's hack was liable to have tried it." It was a decent, respectable living, and definitely not for Al Swearengen.

As railroads pushed west in the post-Civil War era, a traveling "town" that catered to the track layers' vices could be found at the building end of every line. Swearengen came into contact with one such "Hell on Wheels" when the rails passed near Oskaloosa, and it was love at first sight. He abandoned his rig and hit the road, wrote Iverson, "[where] he developed the skills to become a master of ceremonies in the three-ring circus of drinking, gambling and prostitution."

After a year's apprenticeship, Swearengen contracted with William Davie, a distiller in Kentucky, for $12,000 worth of booze and fixtures to equip a saloon of his own in Oskaloosa. It was a risky move because Iowa had just cast off prohibition, but Swearengen forged ahead.

Things did not go well, and by December 1871, Swearengen was "piling up past-due notices," according to Iverson; his salvation came, ironically, when the Iowa State Supreme Court reinstated prohibition. Swearengen thought this a perfect excuse to skip town and leave his Kentucky partner in the lurch.

Davie's lawyers eventually caught up with Swearengen in Denver, where he'd been attempting to disappear. They filed suit, and after a year of legal wrangling the judge delivered a verdict in Davie's favor. Not that it did him much good. Swearengen had already left town, and he next turned up where he wasn't supposed to be. That much might be expected; the surprise is that he was a trusted member of the community.

Custer City was founded while the Black Hills were still part of the Great Sioux Reservation. Whites were prohibited from the area, but that didn't stop Swearengen and others from platting a town. Swearengen opened a saloon/dance hall that was "filled day and night," according to one newspaper account, and whites weren't his only customers, either, as later became apparent.

General George Crook was in charge of the army's effort to keep whites out of the Hills. He gathered the squatters together on August 10, 1875, and ordered them back to Cheyenne. They agreed to go, but asked that a committee be allowed to stay behind and safeguard their property until they were allowed to return. In a head-scratching choice, Al Swearengen was picked to be one of the guardians.

Swearengen might have caused all sorts of mischief in that position, but fortunately for the citizens of Custer City, his sense of responsibility was never tested. When news of gold strikes in the Northern Hills began to percolate through the region, many of the town's residents packed up and left their property to the prairie dogs and coyotes. Swearengen joined the exodus in May of 1876. "He arrived [in Deadwood] on Monday and by the next Saturday he had a dance hall running," according to an account later carried in the *Black Hills Daily Pioneer and Times.*

Meanwhile, Swearengen had been charged with selling liquor to Indians and ordered to stand trial in Yankton, the territorial capital. Needless to say, he didn't appear. A warrant was issued for his arrest, and to his undoubted despair, he was convicted and forced to idle away two months in prison just as thousands of thirsty fortune hunters were streaming into the Black Hills.

Swearengen made it back to Deadwood just as Jack McCall rose from obscurity by gunning down Wild Bill Hickok. He was likely as intrigued as anybody by the murder and subsequent trial, but had more important matters on his mind at that moment: he opened the Cricket Saloon, a permanent structure finished "in grand style," according to a newspaper account, within 10 days of Wild Bill's celebrated passing.

Customers were scarce at first because Deadwood was suffering through one of its periodic outbreaks of smallpox, but once his saloon was up and running, Swearengen immediately set about building an adjoining space for entertainment of various sorts. The first event, staged before his "theater" was even complete, was a prize fight between 'Belfast Chicken' Johnny Marr and 'Cook the Kid' George Latimer. Marr and Latimer went at each other for 52 bare knuckled rounds, and it was all for naught because the referee called it a draw — an outcome which, not coincidentally, allowed Swearengen to keep the prize money.

When Swearengen's Gem Variety Theater formally opened

its doors in the spring of 1877 the *Pioneer* lauded it for being "as neat and tastefully arranged as any place of its kind in the west." There was room for everything dear to his heart: gambling tables, a bar and a small stage, behind which were several bare bones bedrooms where the fallen angels employed by Swearengen practiced the world's oldest profession.

In the two decades of its existence, Swearengen's theater burned with regularity, the first time just three months after it opened. A transparency which had been custom made in Cheyenne caught fire and nearly burned the Gem down. Firemen saved it on that occasion, but two years later Swearengen and the rest of Deadwood weren't so fortunate.

On September 26, 1879, a fire began in the Star Bakery and roared through Deadwood until there was seemingly nothing left to burn. Among the structures consumed was the Gem Theater, a loss that "hit Swearengen doubly hard," wrote Iverson, because he had just refurbished the interior after yet another fire. In the aftermath, Swearengen "promised to rebuild a bigger and better Gem," and for once he kept his word: the larger, more elaborate Gem Theater reopened on New Year's Eve.

As might be expected in a mining camp, the Gem's fare was weighted toward can-can dancers and bawdy skits, with lots of riotous drinking and brawling and dancing to enliven the time between shows. In the course of 20-plus years, however, a surprising range of acts appeared there. Whatever else might be said of him, "Swearengen must be given credit for trying to deliver shows of top-notch quality," wrote Iverson.

Swearengen's most ambitious productions were staged after he hired Harry Montague and company. "Under Montague's tutelage the Gem produced plays of supreme quality," wrote Iverson. His production of the Gilbert & Sullivan musical "The Mikado" was a particular triumph, so much so, "that the owner of the Deadwood Opera House asked if the troupe could perform on his stage." Swearengen declined. He wasn't about to release a show that delivered a better return than almost any mining claim in the Hills: with Montague's hugely popular shows serving as a draw, Swearengen's various enterprises at the Gem took in $5,000 on an average night, and double that on a good one.

The Gem was a cash cow, in modern terms, but no matter how much money Swearengen made it was never enough. Davie, his creditor from Kentucky, finally caught up with him, and after more legal wrangling finally forced him to pay — 10 years after the original debt was incurred. This proved to be Swearengen's business model in Dakota as well. He bilked his partners out of their share of the theater's profits, and didn't settle up until he'd been taken to court; he blamed the Gem's first blaze on Converse & Warren, the firm that manufactured the transparency that caught fire, and didn't pay them until 16 years later.

Swearengen's reputation for dirty dealing must have spread far and wide, yet he could always, quite inexplicably, jawbone suppliers into doing business with him: on one notable occasion a creditor was hauling repossessed furniture out the Gem's front door even as replacement fixtures were coming in the back.

Swearengen treated his employees even worse than his creditors. Women especially suffered. Whether they wanted to or not, nearly all of his female employees were expected to "rustle the boxes," as prostitutes in the small rooms (boxes) upstairs. Women who got out of line or didn't bring in enough money could expect to be set upon by a thuggish "box herder," or the boss himself. "On most days, a segment of the crew at the Gem sported bruises, scratches, scrapes or other maladies in testament of Swearengen's management style," wrote Iverson.

Not many women would tolerate such a life, which obliged Swearengen to find creative ways to replenish his "stock." A muckraking story in the *Black Hills Daily Times* detailed one such scheme, and the headline said it all: "A Den of Prostitution Under the Guise of a Dance Hall, Stocked with Unsuspecting and Innocent Girls, Engaged Through Misrepresentation by its Bestial Proprietor." Swearengen, it seems, had lured 12 teenage girls from Chicago to Deadwood by promising honest work in "a large hotel, theatre and dancing pavilion" he owned. They set out for the Hills with high expectations, "[but] mistrust started soon after departing by reason of certain vile associates."

Fears became reality on their first night at the Gem. Swearengen displayed them on stage like fancy goods in a store window, which reduced several of the terrified girls to tears. Quite unexpectedly, the crowd proved sympathetic and declined to bid on the proffered "merchandise." Such compassion must have dumbfounded Swearengen, who locked the girls in their rooms overnight while he considered the situation. Luckily the town marshal removed the girls from his clutches the next day, and they were home a month later — a rare happy ending for women who wandered into Swearengen's orbit.

This "perfidious transaction," thundered the editor, "[has] disgraced the community and the public is universally outraged ... Deadwood has no need of dens of the Gem order, and the sooner the fact is understood by its proprietor the better it will be for him and the community at large."

Deadwood's outrage, in fact, must have been less than universal because the Gem never lacked for customers thereafter. Not even Prohibition, which was mandated by the state constitution when South Dakota entered the union in 1889, slowed Swearengen. He greased the palms of anybody who might cause trouble, raised his prices to cover the cost and continued operating more or less openly.

By the late 1890s, however, Deadwood had either grown less tolerant of Swearengen and his operation, or he simply grew tired of the game. He closed the Gem's doors and left the bar, the gaming tables and the infamous "boxes" to gather dust. He leased the building out to new operators in 1899, but the Gem Theater wouldn't have a second act. A blaze that reeked of arson broke out in the early morning hours of December

BULLOCK'S FIRE PUMP

DEADWOOD suffered many deadly fires in its early years, but none more devastating than on the night of September 26, 1879. It started in a bakery on Sherman Street and soon engulfed a hardware store, where it ignited eight kegs of blasting powder. Flaming debris flew high and far, spreading the conflagration, and by the time the fire burned itself out more than 100 businesses — including Al Swearengen's infamous Gem Theater — and 75 homes had been reduced to ashes.

Seth Bullock, the soon-to-be-legendary lawman, had seen such a day coming. He had tried to reinvigorate the moribund Deadwood hook and ladder fire company with limited success. Volunteers were hard to recruit. What they needed, Bullock reasoned, was for the fire department to be a source of pride for the men. His solution was to convince the town to invest in top-notch equipment, including the latest steam-powered water pump. Other departments at the time still used old-fashioned hand pumps.

Deadwood had fine fire-fighting equipment available that night, thanks to Bullock. Most of it was consumed by the flames. Only the never-used fire pump survived.

19, and the fire department's ineffective response was either a comedy of errors or part of a conspiracy; by that afternoon there was nothing left.

"The Gem Theater has been a famous landmark in Deadwood for more than 20 years," wrote the *Pioneer's* editor in what sounded like an obituary for both the theater and the man. Everyone who had heard of Deadwood had also heard of Swearengen's establishment, "and to 'do' the Gem was considered a requisite…[for] the traveler who visited Deadwood in early days."

Most of the old-timers who lived through the glorious Days of '76 were forgiven their faults and hailed as heroes when they passed. Not Ellis Albert Swearengen. The *Pioneer* editor's summation concluded, "The Gem Theater has [also] been the object at which every reformer who came into Deadwood has hurled his shaft. For the last 20 years or more it has been held up as a den of infamy and a stumbling block to good morals. Harrowing tales of iniquity, shame and wretchedness; of lives wrecked and fortunes sacrificed; of vice unhindered and esteem forfeited, have been related of the place, and it is known of a verity that they have not all been groundless."

Al Swearengen left Deadwood shortly after the fire, and died five years later in Denver. He was found lying between two railroad tracks, with numerous cuts and scratches on his face and a head wound that looked to have been caused by a large, heavy object. Authorities assumed he was struck while trying to board a moving train.

ON THE WRONG END OF TOWN

DEADWOOD WAS widely known as a place where none of the Ten Commandments were held in especially high regard, but those which frowned upon cheating at cards, fornication, drunkenness, murder and relieving one's neighbor of his gold dust might just as well have been stricken from the Good Book.

No part of town was more responsible for that lawless reputation than the area known as the Badlands, "the raucous, flashy, shabby home of Deadwood's life of sin," wrote Watson Parker in *Deadwood: The Golden Years*. Every vice known to man, from gambling to liquor to opium to prostitutes, could be found at the lower end of Main Street. Al Swearengen's Gem Theater was the most notorious establishment in the neighborhood, but Bella Union, Eureka Hall, Grand Central, Little Bonanza, Old Crow and a dozen more were all equally accomplished at separating a man from his money.

"A cattleman took in the Badlands Saturday," reported the *Black Hills Daily Times* in an all-too-typical story from 1882. "There he fell victim to the blandishments of some of the sirens, who very business-like doped him and rolled him for what money he possessed. A friend . . . later found him nearly dead from the effects of the drugging he got."

Everyone who had been in town longer than a week knew that danger lurked in the Badlands, but greenhorns arrived almost daily and the place prospered for many years. "Tom Hughes, a traveling man who spent Wednesday night seeing the elephant for the first time, claims that he was relieved of his overcoat and several dollars in change," reported the *Times* more than a decade later. "He will not put inquiries as to his loss, remarking philosophically that it was his own fault, as he had no business to visit such places."

Stagecoaches were prime targets for nefarious road agents bent on robbing the occupants. In recent years, coaches have become subjects of nostalgia for western artists like Ron Backer, who painted *Kittie Checks Out Bear Butte* in honor of the 215-mile Medora-to-Deadwood stage line that operated from 1884 to 1886.

CHAPTER 4

Agents of the Road

Stagecoach Robbers, Horse Thieves, Bandits & Other Renegades

A HAGGARD GANG of horsemen rode slowly down Belle Fourche's dusty State Street early on Monday morning, June 28, 1897. The up-and-coming cow town on the northern edge of the Black Hills had grown to become the nation's busiest cattle shipping point, and was readying itself for the work week. The men, slightly hung over, stopped at the Butte County Bank, dismounted and stormed inside.

Chief cashier Art Marble glanced up from his work and was startled to be staring down the barrel of a Colt revolver. The robbers demanded that Marble, his assistant Harry Ticknor and the bank's five customers raise their hands. One of the patrons, Belle Fourche businessman Sam Arnold, was depositing his weekend receipts, and had laid $97 on the teller's counter.

Across the street, Al Giles gazed out the window of his hardware store. He could clearly see men inside the bank with their hands over their heads. Fearing the worst, Giles yelled for help.

The outlaws were caught off guard. One snatched Arnold's $97 and then they all raced to their horses, guns blazing. The gang thundered out of town followed by a riderless horse that had been startled and bolted before its outlaw passenger could climb aboard. The man without a mount searched frantically for another animal. He tried to ride a nearby pack mule out of town, but the stubborn creature refused to move. He fled on foot, and townspeople nabbed him.

Such was the luck of Tom O'Day, who tried his best to be a bona fide Black Hills outlaw, but often found the stars aligned against him. The Hills in the late 19th century attracted some of the country's most unsavory characters. As homesteaders steadily marched west, the frontier reached Dakota Territory in the late 1850s. When George Custer led his expedition to the Black Hills in 1874 and discovered gold, men dreaming of riches flooded the area. They didn't care that they were there illegally. All land west of the Missouri River remained the Great Sioux Reservation. Authorities often turned back wagon trains filled with eager settlers, only to have the evicted parties return in short order. The lure of gold was too much to resist, and the stagecoaches that carried it out of the Hills became easy targets for ruthless road agents.

Some researchers today argue that wild and wooly towns like Deadwood were actually less violent than we have come to believe. In January 1879, the *Black Hills Times* reported just 16 murders had occurred the previous year. But when John Finerty of the *Chicago Tribune* visited Deadwood in 1876, he reported, "a man or two killed every night." The largely lawless Hills saw their share of robberies and murders, perpetrated by some of the West's foulest men and women.

Adams Museum, Deadwood

Tom O'Day roamed the Black Hills with the Sundance Kid's Wild Bunch gang, notorious for botching a bank robbery in Belle Fourche. O'Day was a reliable marksman, but he never killed a soul.

O'Day was born in Pennsylvania in 1862. He moved to Wyoming at age 14, intending to become a cowboy, but he turned to rustling. He met the young and charismatic Harry Longabaugh, soon to be called the Sundance Kid, and joined his Wild Bunch gang.

The group's planned robbery of the Butte County Bank seemed

doomed from the start. Local legend says they designated O'Day to scout the town the day before, but instead he got drunk and returned with no useful information.

The gang proceeded anyway. They rushed inside, hoping to grab as much cash as they could. The obvious first move was to demand patrons throw up their hands, but as Doug Engebretson wrote in *Empty Saddles, Forgotten Names*, cashier Marble later said the gang appeared clueless about what to do next. "They seemed rattled, running from one man to another, telling them to hold up their hands," Marble recalled after the robbery. "They did not seem to do much of anything except run from one man to another." Marble used the moments of indecision to grab a revolver hidden behind the counter, but it misfired when he shot at one of the robbers.

That's when Giles appeared at the door. When he saw the gaggle of gleaming six-shooters, he ran back toward his store with one of the robbers in pursuit. Giles sounded the alarm and the Wild Bunch's plan was abruptly halted. They had no idea that $30,000 sat just a few steps away inside the bank vault.

As his cohorts disappeared toward Sundance Hill, O'Day stood helpless on State Street, wondering what to do next. "Don't shoot the horses!" he blurted at the townspeople in pursuit. "They have one of mine!" The ruse worked briefly, because none of the excited citizens immediately realized that O'Day was part of the gang. Not until his unsuccessful attempt to ride the mule out of Belle Fourche did they realize his true identity. He ran into an outhouse and threw his gun down the hole, but pursuers soon flushed him out.

Townspeople held him for trial, but he was surprisingly acquitted. He moved back to Wyoming and tried to resume his outlaw career. O'Day was later arrested for stealing horses that belonged to future governor B.B. Brooks. He served time in jail, but after his release he decided there must be a better way to make a living. He never ran afoul of the law again, and died in 1930.

O'Day wasn't the only criminal to bumble his way around

the Black Hills. Sam Bass was a Texas ranch hand who came to Dakota with a cattle drive and tried to earn a living by robbing stagecoaches on the Cheyenne to Deadwood route.

Bass was born in Indiana July 21, 1851. He lost both parents by the time he turned 13 and eventually moved to Texas. He joined a group led by Joel Collins that was planning a huge cattle drive to Kansas. When they arrived, they sold the herd for $8,000. Rather than return to Texas with the cattle owners' money, they continued north, arriving in Deadwood in 1876.

Collins opened and briefly ran a dance hall that attracted Deadwood's shadiest citizens. When the cow money ran out, they became road agents. Having no experience working in the Hills, the gang recruited Reddy McKimie, Jim Berry, Tom Nixon and Frank Towle, all outlaws familiar with the country.

Their first robbery attempt was a tragic failure that enraged citizens throughout Dakota Territory. On March 25, 1877, the gang lay in wait at Whitewood Canyon, about two miles south of Deadwood, as the Cheyenne to Deadwood stage rumbled toward them. The masked men thundered from the brush, but

their boisterous shouting startled the coach's six-horse team. The animals bolted, and the trigger-happy McKimie fired a rifle blast into the chest of driver Johnny Slaughter.

The runaway coach sped a half-mile down the trail before the harnesses became tangled. Bass, Collins and their cohorts disappeared into the Hills without an ounce of gold for their efforts.

Citizens and road agents alike expressed their disgust for the brazenness of the robbery. They also lamented the loss of Slaughter, whose father was the city marshal in Cheyenne. Deadwood hosted a

Sam Bass (above) and Joel Collins added locals to their Texas gang when they arrived in the Hills, but their crime spree was hardly lucrative.

huge funeral for the popular Black Hills stage driver before his body was returned to Cheyenne.

Months passed without a robbery along the Cheyenne to Deadwood trail. But the outlaws re-emerged in June 1877, and the trail was no longer safe from crime. A coterie of gangs were likely responsible for the violence, including the Collins-Bass gang. Just before he died, Bass confessed to seven hold-ups along the trail.

If stagecoach robbery was not such a deadly serious business, the career of Sam Bass and his Texas cohorts would go down as among the most comically inept in Black Hills history. They were woefully unprepared for a life of robbery. They were once tipped to a stagecoach rumored to be transporting a large sum of money. When they swarmed the coach, they discovered the only cargo was a load of peaches. Of course, they took the fruit.

Other robberies were absolutely fruitless. Three particular holdups netted $3, $6 and $11. During one holdup, they searched four passengers and found just $30. That led gang member Jack Davis to burst into a tantrum, writes Robert DeArment in *Assault on the Deadwood Stage*. "You are the darnedest set of paupers I ever saw," Davis excoriated the passengers. "What are you traveling for if you don't carry any more money than that? Why, darn it, we fellows will starve if you don't get to doing better."

A brave passenger countered by explaining that the robbers had just placed them in a similar position. He calmly explained that after the holdup, none of them had any money to buy breakfast, and asked for a dollar back. Bass obliged.

Sam Bass' gang stayed in the Black Hills for six months until they realized they weren't cut out for robbing stagecoaches. They moved into Nebraska, where they robbed a Union Pacific gold train near Big Springs in September 1877. The heist produced $60,000, easily their biggest windfall on the Plains.

Bass moved back to Texas and formed a new gang that robbed stagecoaches and trains with limited success. He was researching a job in Round Rock, Texas, when he stopped in a dry goods store to buy tobacco. Texas Rangers recognized the outlaw and shot him. He died two days later on July 21, 1878, his 27th birthday.

A more grisly fate awaited gang member Frank Towle. On September 13, 1878, Towle and his new gang stole a stash of mail sacks from the stage bound for Deadwood. They retreated into the bushes to await the Cheyenne bound coach. When the vehicles met each other, the Deadwood coach's driver told his counterpart about the robbery and warned him that the outlaws might still be around.

Boone May was among the shotgun messengers accompanying the Cheyenne coach. May was a Missouri native who began working for the Cheyenne and Black Hills Stage Company the year before. In three years of guarding stagecoaches between Deadwood and Cheyenne, May was credited with killing four road agents and arresting six more. His reputation as a quick and accurate shot was widely known throughout the Hills.

May and his partner John Zimmerman were ready when Towle and his cohorts attempted to rob the Cheyenne coach. As dusk settled, the two sides exchanged fire and Towle was hit. The gunmen retreated into the Hills as the coach continued.

Three months later, John Irwin, in court and charged with two murders, confessed to his involvement in the Sept. 13 robbery. He claimed his partners buried Towle nearby. May, certain that he fired the shot that killed the desperado, was intent on collecting the handsome reward offered for Towle's apprehension. He returned to the scene, found Towle's grave, dug him up and sliced off his head. He brought the grisly trophy to two county commissions, but both refused to pay the bounty.

When Black Hills residents heard about the killing of Johnny Slaughter and the botched stagecoach robbery, many of them were certain the perpetrator was William Chambers, aka Persimmon Bill. He likely wasn't in the Hills at the time of the robbery, but everyone knew Persimmon Bill was capable of such a crime. He gained his reputation in March 1876, when he cold-bloodedly shot a man in the back and stole $300 from the dead body.

Chambers was born in North Carolina in 1845. He claimed to have fought with both Union and Confederate forces during the Civil War, depending on which side had the upper hand at the time. After the war he went to Wyoming, where he quickly ran afoul of the law. He traveled across Dakota Territory and ended up in Sioux City, where in a booze-fueled fit of rage he shot his own horse and a deputy who was trying to arrest him. Lawmen kicked him out of Sioux City, so he returned to the Black Hills. He and his gang of horse thieves were supposedly headquartered along the Cheyenne to Deadwood stage line near Cheyenne Crossing.

Persimmon Bill was never charged with the murder of H.E. "Stuttering" Brown, division superintendent of the Cheyenne and Black Hills Stage Company, but it was widely believed that he was responsible. In April 1876, Brown visited a ranch along the Cheyenne River while investigating the theft of a team of horses. He found Persimmon Bill and chased him off with a shotgun, threatening to kill him if he didn't leave Dakota Territory. Later that month, Brown was ambushed and killed. Some blamed Indians for the murder, but Luke Voorhees, chairman of the stage company, believed the shooter was Persimmon Bill.

The outlaw is also blamed for the murders of Charles Metz, his wife and their maid. The Metzes had worked as bakers in Custer City and were returning to Laramie with their profits. They were found riddled with arrows, scalped and mutilated in Red Canyon. Once again Indians were blamed for the crime, but locals believed that Persimmon Bill killed the family and made it look like an Indian murder.

He was probably responsible for a few stagecoach robberies, though no concrete proof ever surfaced. He disappeared from the Hills late in the summer of 1878. His fate remains a mystery. Perhaps Boone May killed him when Bill tried to rob a stagecoach but didn't recognize May among the passengers. Maybe a member of his own gang shot him. He may have returned to Tennessee, where he was wanted for an old murder. Or he might have accumulated so much gold through stagecoach robberies that he went back to the South and lived a quiet life until he died.

There long were rumors that Persimmon Bill once ran with Dutch Henry Born, but the pairing seems unlikely. Born became famous as perhaps the country's most successful horse thief, but he also had a knack for recognizing evil men and keeping his distance.

Henry Born wasn't really Dutch. He was born in Wisconsin in 1849 to German immigrant parents, but he got his nickname because he spoke with a heavy German accent. He served briefly with the Seventh Cavalry and was later a civilian scout for Lt. Col. George Custer's outfit in Dakota Territory. But he left before the soldiers' demise at the Battle of the Little Bighorn in 1876. Custer, he later said, was "the meanest man I ever knew."

Born soon became known as the best horse thief in the country. He led a rustling ring across the Great Plains that included as many as 300 men. Born became so adept at the craft that he once stole a horse from a sheriff, and then sold it back to the unsuspecting lawman.

In the 1890s Born homesteaded in Colorado, where he lived quietly and largely law-abidingly with his wife and four children. He died near Pagosa Springs, Colo., in 1921.

Dutch Henry Born became the country's greatest horse thief, leading 300 men who stole Indian ponies and government mules.

As Born settled into his new life in Colorado, the rough and tumble Black Hills was becoming more civilized. Schools, churches and local governments were established in

Black Hills towns, creating a sense of permanence that replaced their boomtown status. Railroads began arriving in the 1880s, gradually making stagecoaches obsolete. The Cheyenne to Deadwood stage took its final run on February 19, 1887. Huge crowds, sensing this was the close of an important era in Western history, turned out to watch.

"The stage holdup has become a memory in the Black Hills, and that only with people who have populated the region for a quarter of a century," wrote Seth Bullock in the *Black Hills Daily Times* in May 1902. "It was one of the incidents of travel that became less and less frequent with the advent of civilization and was completely abolished before the present mode of travel began here. So complete has the evolution been that those who ride into the Black Hills on plush [seats] fail in appreciation of the discomforts and perils that beset the traveler of an earlier period."

So went the era of Black Hills road agents, shotgun messengers, cattle rustlers and horse thieves. Over a century has passed since their crimes shocked and terrified a generation, but their misdeeds are assured a place in Western lore.

SEE FOR YOURSELF
The Adams Museum in downtown Deadwood, the oldest museum in the Black Hills, has excellent exhibits that illustrate the bawdiness, the tragedies and the mysteries of life in Dakota Territory. Phone (605) 578-3724.

CHAPTER 5

Shooting at Saloon No. 10
And the Hanging of Jack McCall

JACK MCCALL STOOD RESOLUTELY atop the wooden gallows. As he gazed toward the east, he peered into the faces of 1,000 men, women and children who had gathered at this spot two miles north of Yankton to witness the first execution in the history of Dakota Territory. He knelt briefly with Father John Daxacher, the Catholic priest who had become his close spiritual adviser during his three months in the Yankton jail. Slowly he stood and kissed a crucifix. Then his world went dark as a black hood covered his head. U.S. Marshal J.H. Burdick gently placed a noose around McCall's neck.

"Wait a moment, Marshal, until I pray," McCall said.

When the condemned man finished, Burdick adjusted the rope. "Draw it tighter, Marshal," McCall requested. Then at 10:15 on the morning of March 1, 1877, the floor beneath McCall's feet disappeared. Witnesses close to the platform heard him quickly blurt, "Oh God," before he dropped out of sight to his death.

McCall was hanged for murdering Wild Bill Hickok in a Deadwood saloon, but his death carried much weight. His arrest, trial, conviction and execution — following an earlier trial at which he was acquitted — demonstrated the territorial government's authority to control the Black Hills country. Deadwood in 1876 was still part of the Great Sioux Reservation. White settlers were technically not allowed on land west of the Missouri River. Since no legitimate court held jurisdiction over the mining community deep in Indian country, it was as if McCall's original trial, held before a hastily assembled miners' court, had never happened. His death has also fed countless stories about McCall's motive, and whether or not he acted alone.

Hardly any details survive that describe McCall's life before he put a bullet in Hickok's head. He was born in Jefferson County, Kentucky in 1852 or 1853, and grew up with three sisters. At some point, he moved west to become a buffalo hunter. When he wandered into Deadwood in the spring of 1876, he claimed to be a stagecoach driver, and may have found work as a freight driver.

On August 1, 1876 he was in Nuttall and Mann's Saloon No. 10 when a man got up to leave a poker game. McCall took his seat and found himself playing with Wild Bill Hickok, whose reputation as a rogue lawman and gunfighter was widely known.

It was Hickok's lucky day. When the game ended, McCall owed Wild Bill $16.25, all the money he had in his wallet. "Did I break you?" Hickok asked.

"Yes," McCall curtly replied.

Hickok offered McCall 75 cents to buy a meal, but he refused the money and left.

No one knows with certainty if McCall vowed vengeance after his humiliating defeat, but he nonchalantly slipped into Saloon No. 10 the following afternoon. Hickok was again playing poker, this time with Carl Mann, Charles Rich and former riverboat Captain William Massie. The quartet played at a table in the center of the room. Hickok sat with his back to the door, unusual for a man who always wanted to be aware of his surroundings. It allowed McCall to slip virtually unnoticed to a position behind Hickok.

Wild Bill's gambling luck was changing. "The old duffer," Hickok remarked during the game, referring to Massie. "He broke me on the hand."

Those were Hickok's final words. McCall approached the table and stopped about three feet behind Hickok. He leveled his Sharps revolver with a piece of buckskin around the stock at the back of Hickok's head and fired.

"Damn you, take that!" McCall shouted as the shot cracked through the saloon. The slug smashed through Hickok's skull, ripped through his right cheek and lodged in Massie's right wrist. For a moment, silence pervaded Saloon No. 10. Hickok sat motionless, then fell from his chair. Patrons fled. McCall backed toward the exit, waving his gun and yelling, "Come on, you sons of bitches!" He tried to shoot bartender Sam Young and George Shingle, but the gun misfired.

McCall fled down the alley behind Saloon No. 10. He tried to steal a horse, but its owner had loosened the saddle because of the heat, and McCall tumbled to the ground as he tried to mount the animal. He ran and hid in a butcher shop until a well-armed crowd found and extracted him.

Then the swiftness of frontier justice took over. Since no established court held sway over Deadwood, its citizens settled legal matters among themselves in miners' courts. For the accused, these speedy trials ended in one of two ways: hanging or acquittal and immediate eviction from the Hills.

McCall's captors led him to James McDaniels' Deadwood Theatre the following day, where the names of 12 jurors, some of whom happened to be friends of McCall's, were drawn from a hat. The trial commenced at 2 p.m. McCall claimed the shooting was justified because Hickok had murdered his brother in Kansas. "Wild Bill threatened to kill me if I crossed his path," McCall reportedly told the court. "I am not sorry for what I have done. I would do the same thing over again."

Infamy came to Jack McCall, a quiet drifter, after he killed Wild Bill Hickok.

The jury, comprised of miners and businessmen, deliberated for two hours, and by 6 p.m. returned with a verdict: not guilty. Such prompt administrations of justice were common in Deadwood, and led the editor of the *Black Hills Pioneer* to write, "Should it ever be our misfortune to kill a man, we would simply ask that our trial take place in some of the mining camps of these hills."

Oddly, McCall stayed in Deadwood for a few days after the trial, purportedly to check on mining claims. Eventually he headed west and surfaced in Laramie, Wyo., where he bragged about killing Wild Bill. But his story began changing. He told some people that Hickok had indeed murdered his brother. On another occasion he claimed he shot Wild Bill because he was angry about losing the poker game.

Lawmen soon heard of McCall's presence in town. They had no confidence in the verdict rendered by a ragtag jury in Deadwood, and thought that only an established court in Dakota Territory could properly dispense justice. Territorial officials agreed. They declared double jeopardy did not apply and issued an arrest warrant. Federal authorities apprehended McCall on August 29 and transported him to Yankton, capital of Dakota Territory, to await a new trial.

McCall spent the next three months in jail. His cellmate was an accused murderer named McCarty. The two attempted an escape one day in November. They assaulted the jailer and were walking out the door just as Marshal Burdick and a deputy were entering.

The miner-turned-killer was indicted at the Yankton courthouse on October 18. Because he couldn't afford an attorney, Judge Granville Bennett appointed Oliver Shannon and Gen. William Henry Harrison Beadle to the defense team.

McCall's trial began on December 5. When Marshal Burdick escorted the prisoner into the courtroom on the trial's opening day, the *Yankton Press and Dakotan* reporter assigned to cover the proceedings described the heavily shackled defendant as "an evil looking man young in years but apparently old in sin."

The first day involved jury selection in the morning, and only a smattering of spectators dotted the gallery. But when eyewitness testimony began that afternoon, it was clear that residents in the 16-year-old city on the banks of the Missouri River were deeply interested. The courtroom was filled as George Shingle, Carl Mann and William Massie took the stand. All identified McCall as the sole murderer of Wild Bill Hickok.

During McCall's time in Yankton, his story continued changing. He claimed he was drunk at the time of the shooting. He also tried to blame a man named John Varnes, whom he said had paid him to assassinate Hickok over a disputed poker game in Denver.

The Yankton trial didn't proceed as swiftly as Deadwood's, but it still finished quickly. Testimony and closing arguments concluded after noon on December 6. At 7 p.m., Judge P.C. Shannon dismissed the jury for deliberations. The 12 men returned shortly before midnight and announced their guilty verdict. On January 3, 1877, McCall was sentenced to death by hanging, scheduled for March 1.

McCall seemed resigned to his sentence, but as he awaited death in the Yankton jail, his lawyers tried everything they could to overturn the decision. Shannon and Beadle lobbied for a new trial, arguing that Deadwood was outside the jurisdiction of Dakota Territory. They took their case all the way to the territorial Supreme Court, which denied their request. The lawyers made a final appeal to outgoing President Ulysses S. Grant, hoping to lessen the sentence to life in prison, but Grant refused to interfere.

March 1 dawned cold and drizzly in Yankton. Inside the jail, McCall met privately with Father Daxacher as Marshal Burdick and other officers and clergy stood nearby. At 9 a.m., Burdick read the death warrant aloud. McCall, finally freed from his shackles, shared a few more words with Father Daxacher.

At 9:30, the large crowd gathered outside caught a glimpse of McCall as he left the jail and climbed into a light carriage. Phil Faulk, a writer for the *Press and Dakotan*, rode with McCall to the gallows. "This mournful train, bearing its living victim to the grave, was preceded and followed by a long line of vehicles of every description, with hundreds on horseback and on foot, all leading north, out through Broadway," Faulk wrote. "The rain which was falling had moistened the earth and deadened the sound of the carriage wheels. Not a word was spoken during the ride two miles to the school section north of the Catholic cemetery. McCall still continued to bear up bravely, even after the gallows loomed in full view."

They arrived promptly at 10 a.m. Deputy Marshal Henry Ash escorted McCall, who was dressed entirely in black, to the platform. The wooden gallows measured 8 by 10 feet. The floor where McCall stood was 8 feet off the ground. The area from the platform to the ground was completely enclosed, so when the trap was sprung and McCall disappeared, no one saw the moment when his neck snapped, and the rope slowly squeezed the life from him.

Twelve minutes later, two doctors entered the enclosed portion of the gallows and pronounced McCall dead. His hands were clenched and blue. One still clutched a crucifix. After another 10 minutes, McCall's body was cut down, placed in

SEE FOR YOURSELF

Visitors to Deadwood remain enamored with the story of Wild Bill Hickok's death, so re-enactors stage the shooting, followed by the capture and trial of Jack McCall regularly throughout the summer. Call (800) 999-1876 for information. North of Yankton, a historical marker stands on the spot where McCall was executed. Find it near the south entrance to the Human Services Center on Highway 50. Another marker can be found downtown, attached to an old, three-story brick building at 3rd & Capitol in which McCall was tried.

a walnut coffin and buried virtually on the spot in a corner of the Catholic cemetery.

His remains lay there undisturbed for four years. In 1881, the federal government chose that spot as the site of the new Dakota Hospital for the Insane. When Father Valentine Sommereisen, Yankton's first resident priest, established the tiny cemetery years earlier, he hadn't obtained the proper permissions, so the land wasn't officially designated as a cemetery. The bodies buried there, including McCall's, had to be relocated. When his coffin was opened, onlookers discovered he had been buried with the noose still around his neck.

McCall was moved to the Catholic portion of the city cemetery. Over the years, his gravesite became a tourist attraction, much to the chagrin of the city's Catholic leaders. Local historians say that in the 1930s, Father Lawrence Link, who served Yankton's Sacred Heart Church from 1895 until his death in 1946, supervised a third relocation of McCall's remains. This time, he was buried in an unmarked grave in Sacred Heart Cemetery, where he lies today.

When McCall died, the truth behind what happened at Saloon No. 10 in Deadwood on August 2, 1876 died with him. As he counted his final hours in the Yankton jail, McCall had prepared a letter, which he intended to give the *Press and Dakotan* the morning of the hanging. But the night before his death, McCall destroyed it. Historians wonder if it contained his true motives or if it was simply another attempt to distance himself from responsibility.

The shared legend of Jack McCall and Wild Bill Hickok grew through the years. Visitors to Deadwood stop at the place once occupied by Saloon No. 10. They also pay respects at Wild Bill's grave in Mount Moriah Cemetery. For years Yankton leaders advertised their city's connection to history with a large roadside billboard that read, "We haven't hung anyone since Jack McCall!" The sign is gone, but McCall remains, hidden somewhere in the cemetery on Douglas Avenue, and his legend will survive for centuries.

Steve and Charlie Utter at Wild Bill Hickok's gravesite

THE BURIAL OF WILD BILL

To his last, best friend, Charlie Utter (Colorado Charlie)

Under the sod in the prairie-land
　　We have laid him down to rest,
With many a tear from the sad, rough throng
　　And the friends he loved the best;
And many a heartfelt sigh was heard
　　As over the earth we trod,
And many an eye was filled with tears
　　As we covered him with the sod.

Under the sod in the prairie-land
　　We have laid the good and the true—
An honest heart and a noble scout
　　Has bade us a last adieu.
No more his silvery laugh will ring,
　　His spirit has gone to God;
Around his faults let Charity cling
　　While you cover him with the sod.

Under the sod in the land of gold
　　We have laid the fearless Bill;
We called him Wild, yet a little child
　　Could bend his iron will.
With generous heart he freely gave
　　To the poorly clad, unshod—
Think of it, pards—of his noble traits—
　　While you cover him with the sod.

Under the sod in Deadwood Gulch
  You have laid his last remains;
No more his manly form will hail
  The red man on the plains.
And, Charley, may Heaven bless you!
  You gave him a "bully good send;"
Bill was a friend to you, pard,
  And you were his last, best friend.

You buried him 'neath the old pine tree,
  In that little world of ours,
His trusty rifle by his side—
  His grave all strewn with flowers;
His manly form in sweet repose,
  That lovely silken hair
I tell you, pard, it was a sight,
  That face so white and fair!

And while he sleeps beneath the sod
  His murderer goes free,
Released by a perjured, gaming set,
  Who'd murder you and me—
Whose coward hearts dare never meet
  A brave man on the square.
Well, pard, they'll find a warmer clime
  Than they ever found out there.

Hell is full of just such men;
  And if Bill is above to-day,
The Almighty will have enough to do
  To keep him from going away—
That is, from making a little scout
  To the murderers' home below;
And if old Peter will let him out,
  He can clean out the ranch, I know

Capt. Jack Crawford, the "poet scout" of the Black Hills, wrote this poem about the death of Wild Bill Hickok. The Irish-born immigrant was an illiterate Union soldier who learned to read and write from a Sister of Charity while recuperating from injuries. He became a newspaper reporter. He arrived in the Black Hills in 1875 as a journalist, but was also appointed captain of the Black Hills Rangers. He worked as a scout and became known both for his skill with a pen and for being a teetotaler, a rare characteristic. After several years in the Black Hills, he signed on with Buffalo Bill Cody's Wild West Show.

Hill City brothel owner Bismarck Anne, right, posing with a woman
nicknamed Crazy Horse.

Photo courtesy of the Journey Museum

CHAPTER 6

Fallen Angels

WOMEN WERE as scarce as gold in the Black Hills, and equally desirable. For that matter, ladies were few in number throughout the entire Dakota Territory. Frontier towns and mining communities from Yankton to Deadwood were simply too uncivilized for all but the most adventurous or desperate women.

Soldiers and other government officials generally left their wives and children at home before serving in Dakota Territory, or they settled them in Sioux City, Iowa, or some other "eastern city" before entering the wild country.

Yankton, the first territorial capital, became home to steamboat crews, army camp followers, gamblers, gypsies and risk-loving businessmen trying their luck on the frontier. Houses of ill repute lined Levee Street near the river to cater to the men. As part of the cost of doing business, madams regularly showed up in court to pay fines for their illegal transactions. The local *Press and Dakotan* wrote in detail of each sentence the madams garnered. Residents knew Levee Street's madams by name, and should have thanked them for filling the city coffers — they once paid $2,600 in prostitution fines during a seven-month period. Local editors termed the penalties "the wages of sin."

Marie Briggs was Yankton's most prominent madam. She arrived in the early 1870s and managed to survive in a competitive business climate on Levee Street for 20 years. Her establishment came under special scrutiny when the newspaper reported that a 12-year-old runaway girl was living in the brothel.

Readers imagined the worst, but an investigation soon revealed that the girl was working as a chambermaid for $2.50 a week and was being treated quite kindly.

Still, Briggs and her fellow madams were never welcomed in polite Yankton society — even though their livelihoods depended on the town fathers' affections. Another madam named Doyle left town for greener pastures, and afterward she was scolded by the newspaper for neglecting to pay some bills. In a letter to the editor, Doyle said that she would happily pay her creditors if certain men in town would settle their bills with her — and she added that she would be willing to identify them if it would help to clarify the situation. The matter was soon forgotten.

Briggs survived in the trade longer than most, and when she died in 1893 the *Press and Dakotan* had a few kind words: "She was a woman of kindly impulses, considerable intelligence and wide acquaintance," wrote the editor. "Her fortune is said to amount to $35,000."

Across the territory in Rapid City, another powerful madam operated houses of ill repute for 40 years. Amy Helen Dorothea Bolshaw was born in 1868, in Liverpool, England, and emigrated to America with her parents while still in diapers. She grew to be a beautiful young woman by all accounts, and in the usual course of such things she might have married a nice young man, raised a family and lived out her years as a respectable citizen. For reasons known only to her, Dora chose a different path. At the tender age of 15 she began working as a dance hall girl in Rapid City.

Dora arrived in the Black Hills in the early 1880s, after the gold rush era had passed into legend, but the freewheeling mining camp culture was still alive: there were saloons, dance halls and brothels galore across the region. Dora soon gradu-

Photo courtesy of the Adams Museum, Deadwood

DuFran was a mother, madam and, according to her obituary, a do-gooder.

ated from being an ordinary "soiled dove," as prostitutes were referred to in print, to running her own sporting house. Over the next 40 years she operated houses in Belle Fourche, Lead, Deadwood and Rapid City.

While living in Deadwood, Dora married Joseph DuFran, a prospector turned gambler. As occupations go, madam and card sharp weren't normally conducive to long-term relationships, but the two were still together when Joseph died in 1909, and they apparently raised at least one child together. Dora's imposing tombstone in Mount Moriah Cemetery has "Mother" chiseled across the top. Her gravesite is also marked by four urns, possibly representing the four houses she operated in her lifetime.

Dora's most celebrated establishment was in Belle Fourche. She advertised it as a spot for "Three D's — Dining, Drinking and Dancing," and less plausibly as, "a place where you can bring your mother." Cowboys and other customers knew better, however.

After Joseph passed away, Dora relocated to Rapid City, where the Coney Island brothel she opened in 1909 became a civic institution. Various madams kept it running well into the 1950s despite the location's drawbacks, which became apparent one rainy night. Earl Cox, who grew up on a ranch near Sturgis, recounted the oft-told tale as he heard it from old-timers while he was growing up.

"Dora's Coney Island bordello in the middle of Rapid Creek was reached by a [foot]bridge," Cox wrote. "History tells us that one night a flash flood took out the bridge and stranded the movers and shakers … who were meeting at Dora's. When the water subsided at daylight the city dads saw a chilling sight. On the riverbank opposite Coney Island stood the grim-faced wives of the errant businessmen … carrying rolled-up umbrellas and other weapons."

Dora passed away in 1934 at age 69, old enough, apparently, for her many years to be reviewed with some kindness. "Dora DuFran Served Suffering Humanity" was the headline on her lengthy obituary in the *Rapid City Journal*. The newspaper reported that Dora had served as a midwife to destitute women. She was generous to the less fortunate. She nursed the victims of the 1918 influenza epidemic. She turned her home into a private hospital, open to those who couldn't afford to be treated elsewhere. No mention was made of her entertainment career.

Bismarck Anne of Keystone was not as disposed toward community service as Dora DuFran, and if she had stayed in Keystone, she wouldn't have received a glowing obituary. Anne Parks was a dark-haired beauty when she worked at brothels in Custer and Hill City. But by the time she'd earned enough to have her own house of ill repute in Keystone, named The Palace, she was not-so-pretty and the local women despised her.

Above all, they frowned upon her recruitment of local farm girls to work in her brothel. Martha Linde's book, *Rushmore's Golden Valleys,* reported that the women of Keystone once created a disturbance across town to attract Anne's attention. While she was away, they and a minister rescued three of the girls and hastily married them to the first three men they could find.

Alice Tubbs, known as Poker Alice, was also a thorn to polite society. She opened her infamous Sturgis sporting house after her second husband, Warren Tubbs, passed away. Every soldier at nearby Fort Meade knew he could get drunk, hire a woman and gamble away a month's pay at Alice's establishment. Somewhat surprisingly, this volatile brew of entertainments boiled up a tragedy just once. There are two conflicting versions of the event, and they agree on only one point: Alice shot and killed a cavalry sergeant. He was unarmed, but a jury concluded she had acted in self-defense.

Of course, it had to be so. Poker Alice was a bit of a civic embarrassment, certainly, but she had a good heart. She even taught her girls Bible lessons on Sundays.

Alice's matronly style was quite the opposite of brothel owner Al Swearengen, who gained notoriety a century later in the HBO series *Deadwood.* Swearengen had a harsh reputation but he had the backing of Deadwood's most prominent citizens, and his Gem Theater was a popular hangout in the mining camp. He staged bawdy shows, kept a stable of prostitutes and sold countless barrels of overpriced whiskey. The ruthless solicitor was notorious for luring women to the Hills with promises of reputable employment, then forcing them into prostitution. Scarcely a month passed at the Gem without some despairing woman's suicide.

One of Calamity Jane's first jobs in Deadwood was as a Swearengen girl. James McLaird wrote in his book *Calamity Jane,* "She immediately became a dance hall celebrity. Those who assume she was too dissolute and masculine to be attractive missed essential qualities of her character."

Not all dance hall girls were prostitutes, but all were expected to dance. The dancing didn't cost any money, but the man was then obligated to buy the girl and himself an expensive drink at the bar. As the evening progressed the dancing got sloppier and the proprietor got richer. At the end of the night, the owner would share his profits with the girls.

Calamity Jane also was hired by Swearengen to travel to Sidney, Neb., to recruit women for the Gem. Journalist Leander Richardson, who spent five days in Deadwood writing an article titled "A Trip in the Black Hills" for *Scribner's Monthly,* reported that Calamity Jane kept her own house of ill repute, and became the rival of Kitty Arnold.

Not much is known about Miss Arnold, except that she arrived in Deadwood with the caravan of Wild Bill Hickok, Charlie Utter and Calamity Jane. She was a dance hall girl for Swearengen, but there are accounts of her eventually owning her own parlor house. Richardson wrote that she was the prettiest and most elegant girl in Deadwood, in stark contrast to Calamity Jane, who often dressed in men's clothing and a large cowboy hat. But, Richardson reported, Calamity Jane could outride, outdrink and outshoot Arnold, and proved it at least once by shooting out the windows in her rival's establishment.

Richardson witnessed Arnold's outgoing personality while attending a play called *The Streets of New York in the Mining Camp.* The audience was mostly male, but there were a "few mining camp damsels." Kitty sashayed into the theater in a fancy yellow silk dress with a long train and low neckline and a cheap cigar in her mouth. She sat down and offered the gentleman next to her a cigar. He, in turn, offered her some tobacco, which she graciously accepted. The show commenced. Richardson noted the play was horribly performed. The audience loved it, however, and he later wrote:

There is a sound of expectoration and a voice is heard that penetrates to every part of the building — the voice of Kitty Arnold, the belle of Deadwood City. It says, in the accents of one whose finer sensibilities have been trifled with: "Oh, hell! That was a put-up job."

For a part of an instant the big, bare auditorium with its canvas roof is as still as death. Then there is an outburst of yells, cheers and wild laughter, such as one does not often hear. In the course of this hilarious turmoil, which dies away and then rises again and again, Miss Arnold hastily withdraws from the theater, and at least a third of the audience goes with her, putting in a considerable portion of the night carousing in her establishment.

Richardson also wrote of Eleanor Dumont, who similarly arrived in Deadwood with the Hickok/Utter delegation. She was a quick witted, charming dark beauty. As a successful card dealer with a reputation for fairness, she charmed men into playing at her table. She came from California but led a nomadic life, settling where she could make a living. As she got older, her activities became more unsavory; she became a madam in the 1860s and at times turned tricks herself when she was out of money. By the time she became a Deadwood madam, her looks were fading and a dark fuzz on her upper lip had grown, giving her the name Madame Moustache. Her business in Deadwood was short lived, and she moved on to other towns to make a living. She died in 1879, committing suicide by overdosing on morphine. She had played poorly that night, ending the evening in debt.

Another Deadwood madam was Mollie Johnson, the flashy "Queen of the Blondes" who employed three fellow blondes to both work as prostitutes and run houses for her in Deadwood. She arrived in Deadwood in 1878 and was known for throwing lively parties and dances. Her house was near the Empire Bakery, where a huge fire started in 1879 that destroyed much of

Deadwood's main street. Johnson reportedly began to rebuild the next day and was soon back to business.

Deadwood's lively Chinatown branched off from Main Street and meandered north. News of the gold rush attracted the Chinese to either work in the mines or cater to the miners. Chinatown housed around 200 people and included grocery stores, restaurants, gambling halls, opium dens, bakeries, laundries and boarding houses. Chinatown was a large part of the Deadwood community from about 1877 to 1930. While most of the Chinese immigrants were men, a thriving prostitution trade sprung up that was frequented by Chinese and whites alike.

All the girls of Deadwood's famed Chinatown were charming and smiling, but none as beautiful as Yellow Doll, who entertained with a style that captivated all the miners. She came to Deadwood in 1876 from San Francisco. Prostitution was condoned both in the Chinese immigrant culture and the all-male mining communities of the West, and Yellow Doll was a respected and well-liked young lady. She was so popular with the men, both Asian and American, that the other saloon girls became quite envious.

Their resentment may have been a factor in Yellow Doll's early and violent death. Her lifeless and bloodied body was found hacked to pieces by a madman (madwoman?) in her room above the saloon. Police ruled out a murder prompted by robbery, because all of the young beauty's jewels and possessions were intact in her fine living quarters. Her murder has never been solved, and her burial site is unknown.

Fanny Hill opened a house just down the road in Lead in 1897. *Deadwood Magazine* wrote that she was arrested 136 times throughout the next 14 years, and paid over $10,000 in fines. When her house opened a Deadwood newspaper announced the housewarming party:

Fanny Hill, well known in the Tenderloin district of Lead, will soon take possession of the Miller block on Mill Street and will give a grand reception that night. Many of the prominent

Pam Holliday was one of Deadwood's last madams.

END OF AN ERA

Prostitution has been illegal since territorial days, but the trade thrived in Deadwood until the 1980s.

State and county officials had been working for decades to shut down brothels in Deadwood, but the town turned a blind eye. Deadwood officials had a long history of fining madams and giving them jail time, but not shutting down establishments.

Michael Trump, in *Raiding Deadwood's Bad Lands*, wrote that prostitution was overlooked because it was a crucial part of Deadwood nightlife that drew thousands to the little mountain town. Pressure from Lawrence County residents might have forced the State's Attorney to take action, but few complaints were ever filed.

"The town of Deadwood continued to embrace their brothels because they symbolized the last remaining element of the wild western town its promoters claimed it to be and because Deadwood's citizens had come to accept and depend on the houses as a viable economic resource," wrote Trump.

Deadwood prostitution came to an abrupt end in 1980 in a surprise federal raid that shut down four establishments in one day, including the infamous Pam's Purple Door. Pam Holliday raised money for lawyers' fees by holding a large auction that featured racy memorabilia.

A "Save our Tail" parade was a last hoorah for Deadwood prostitutes. About 30 prostitutes and their supporters rode up and down Main Street, proclaiming support for the brothels.

Deadwood Madam Bea Wheeler (center) with some of her working girls in the 1940s.

Photos: Adams Museum, Deadwood

57

businessmen claim to have received invitations, but chances are but few will join in the revelries of the occasion.

The *Deadwood Daily Independent* predicted that unless Fanny, who was in her late 20s at the time, kept strict order in the house it would not be open for long. Hill did just that and her house was a lively institution in Lead for many years.

CHAPTER 7

Hangman's Hill
An Infamous Day in Rapid City

LOUIS "RED" Curry and A.J. "Doc" Allen were horse thieves. Of that there is no doubt. On June 20, 1877, they were caught near Rapid City with two horses that belonged to the Salisbury-Gilmer stagecoach line, and unfortunately for them, vigilante justice was nothing if not swift and decisive. They were hanged by the neck before they saw another sunrise.

Curry and Allen were disreputable characters; there was a better than fair chance they had already gotten away with other crimes. They were caught with the stolen horses and admitted their guilt. What was the point of waiting for a judge to sentence them to hang? That's how the grimly self-righteous lynch mob might have justified their actions.

If only the crowd hadn't hanged a third, innocent man.

There are several accounts of this infamous case of vigilante justice. John S. McClintock came to Deadwood in 1876 and stayed until his demise in 1942. He published *Pioneer Days in the Black Hills* shortly before he died, and his outraged indictment of the vigilantes in the chapter "Hanging Of An Innocent Boy At Rapid City" was the product of personal recollection and the patient collecting of information over the years.

Mildred Fielder depended on hearsay for a generous helping of conversation and dramatic detail in her retelling of the tale for *True West* magazine in 1964, but she also quoted extensively from contemporary newspaper accounts and testimony before the coroner's jury that looked into the matter. Her reputation as a well-regarded authority on Black Hills history — she wrote more than 20 books on subjects from gold mining to the region's native fruits — gave weight to what might otherwise be dismissed as historical fiction.

Mont Hawthorne was in Rapid City at the time of the lynching, and years later he recalled the aftermath in *Them Was the Days: An American Saga of the '70s*. Robert J. Casey spent more time berating the residents of Rapid City for their attitudes than he did on the actual lynching when he wrote about it in *The Black Hills*. Works Progress Administration (WPA) writers from the 1930s and various other sources provide a few occasionally contradictory particulars, yet none of the accounts sufficiently capture the dreadful reality.

James "Kid" Hall, a boy of 18 or perhaps younger, was on the trail between Deadwood and Rapid City on that afternoon of June 20. He was all alone and newly arrived to the region, one of thousands of young men looking to strike it rich in the Black Hills. McClintock and Fielder wrote that he was afoot, a most unusual mode of transportation considering the country and a telling detail. When Curry and Allen came along, both on horseback and leading two spare animals, he happily accepted their offer to ride.

Mont Hawthorne was a little younger than Hall when he reached Rapid City with his father, an entrepreneur headed for Deadwood with two wagonloads of flour that he hoped to sell at exorbitant prices. In Hawthorne's recollection, James Hall came from Austin, Minn., to the Black Hills with his father. All of the promising claims near Deadwood had been taken, so the elder Hall moved on to Yellowstone while the younger made his way back to Minnesota. He was riding his own horse, which his father had purchased from a man near Sturgis, when he fell in with Curry and Allen.

(Hawthorne and McClintock both believed Hall's real name was Mansfield. Most other accounts refer to him as Hall, however, so for clarity's sake that name will be used here.)

Curry and Allen were leery about going on to Rapid City, where the branded horses might be recognized. They settled down for the night in a grove of trees on what is now known as Cowboy Hill, northwest of Rapid. They invited Hall to join them, which seems quite neighborly for a pair of lowlifes, but Curry and Allen may have had an ulterior motive: the presence of a third man might make their extra animals easier to explain.

Meanwhile, David Marble, Howard Worth and others were in the area cutting logs. They spied the group and mistook them for Indians, so they bolted for town to raise the alarm. Sheriff Frank Moulton decided that the best defense was to take the fight to the enemy, so he formed a posse.

Moulton and his posse surrounded the grove on Cowboy Hill, then charged in and rudely roused Curry, Allen and Hall from their dreams. "With a quick estimate of the situation, [a fourth man, Ed Powell] leaped aboard a horse and got away," wrote Casey.

Curry and Allen were known as dissolute sorts. Finding them with extra animals made Deputy Harry Waite and the rest of the arresting party suspicious. Then the Deadwood stage happened along carrying Ed Cook, superintendent of the Salisbury-Gilmer line. He identified two of the animals as having been stolen from the company's barn in Crook City. That was Fielder's version. Cook didn't identify the stolen horses until later that day, in Rapid City, according to Casey.

Allen must have figured his fate was sealed when Cook identified the horses, but he tried to defend himself. "Stage horses look like any other kind of horses in the dark," he blurted. "How come your outfit don't keep them stabled a little better?"

With that admission, some of the posse wanted to save time and string the trio up, for no character in the West was more loathsome than a horse thief. Sheriff Moulton kept control of the situation, however, and insisted that the three would stand trial in Deadwood. As they were being tied up, Curry and Allen insisted that Hall wasn't with them, but the posse didn't buy it.

There was no jail in Rapid City, so the prisoners were locked up in the Breman & Nicholson granary. Someone fetched Justice of the Peace Robert Burleigh. While it's doubtful that this exchange from Fielder's story constitutes a literal record, it seems true to the spirit of what might charitably be called Burleigh's approach to judicial process.

"What's the trouble here?" Burleigh asked.

"Horse thieves." The word was spat into the air [by one of the posse]. "We caught them with the goods out there in the canyon."

"Guilty?" Burleigh asked [Curry and Allen].

"That's right," Doc said.

Red nodded, but added loudly, "We might be guilty but this kid's not."

Eyes were turned toward James Hall, and someone laughed but it didn't sound funny.

"Guilty?" Burleigh asked the boy.

"No, sir," the kid said quietly. "No, sir, I'm not a horse thief."

Again and again, in every account, Curry and Allen are shown to be remarkably cooperative and conscientious for hardened criminals. They readily admit their guilt, and with their next breath they try to get Hall off the hook. John Jennack, who was a boy of 16 when he witnessed the hangings, remembered the pair pleading for Hall's life while the hangmen's ropes were around their necks.

Hall is depicted as unfailingly humble and polite by Fielder. That is at odds with what Casey gathered from talking to witnesses many years after the events. "Kid Hall was angry and noisy and undiplomatic," wrote Casey. "He told the sheriff and four deputies face to face that they were 'skates,' 'rubes,' and 'gazebos,' and added that they had been born out of wedlock." This would seem an imprudent course of action when in the hands of a lynch mob, "and one wonders how much the Kid's studied effort to direct resentment against himself had to do with his subsequent [hanging]. The posse, readily joining in the vocal brawl, seemed to have forgotten Allen and Curry."

Justice of the Peace Burleigh disappears until after the hanging in Fielder's account; he convened a hearing that night, said

Casey. "According to some respected historians, this arraignment was conducted in the International Hotel, which hadn't yet been put up," wrote Casey. No written record was kept, "and afterward there was some disagreement, particularly between 'Judge' Burleigh and Henry Curry, who had come looking for his son's body, concerning what really went on. Burleigh declared that Allen and Curry had admitted stealing the horses but had exonerated Kid Hall of any crime except swearing at the deputy sheriffs." Burleigh's admission throws an unfavorable light on him: a more forceful and conscientious figure might have succeeded in saving Hall, at least, but Burleigh was apparently not such a man.

What happened when and who said what that night will never be known. Too many people had too much to hide. "By noon the next day most of the people who had been in the court weren't talking any," according to Casey.

Sheriff Moulton returned the prisoners to the granary and detailed four men, including Deputy Billy Smith, to guard them. Burleigh and Moulton then retired from the scene, either unaware of or willfully ignoring the trouble that was brewing.

Members of the posse and other gadabouts retired to a nearby saloon to discourse on the subject of horse thieves and justice. "Considerable interest was manifested that night over the affair," according to material gathered by the WPA writers. "Around the post office spectators heard the phrase, 'Whiskey drinks are free tonight, Stage Company's treat,' passing from mouth to ear."

Such generosity may not have been occasioned solely in gratitude for the recovery of two stolen horses. There was a stagecoach robbery about a week before the hanging. Before that, W. McLachlan, a teamster hauling supplies for the stage line, had gone missing and was presumed to have been murdered. Officials of Salisbury-Gilmer may have genuinely believed Curry and Allen were responsible for both crimes, or they might have seized the opportunity to send a message to other would-be thieves. Either way, a drunken mob was the perfect instrument. After some hours of discussion the inebriated vigilantes decided to act.

In his appearance before a coroner's jury, convened the next day almost literally in the hanging tree's shadow atop the prominence that soon became known as Hangman's Hill, Smith testified as to what happened next.

"[Deputy William E. Smith] said that on the morning of the 21st day of June, 1877, he was in charge of prisoners confined in warehouse of Breman & Nicholson. That on said morning between the hours of one and three a party of masked men between 15 and 20 in number, approached him while standing at the door of said prison and demanded him to open the door. He refused to do so. They then demanded the key to the door ... He was then seized by numbers of the party who overpowered him by force, the door was then opened and about one half the party went in and demanded the arms of the inside guards, told the prisoners to get up and put on their boots.

"'I saw no more of them until this morning, between the hours of five and six o'clock. I saw the bodies of the prisoners swinging from yonder tree.'"

To make matters even more gruesome, it was later discovered that the lynch mob didn't know their business very well. They didn't tie a proper hangman's knot or judge the ropes' length correctly; the prisoners' falls didn't break their necks and instantaneously kill them, as was supposed to happen. Instead, they fell and their feet just touched the ground, leaving them to slowly strangle to death.

"[Residents] of the other Hills towns referred to the worthy citizens of Rapid as 'stranglers' for a long time after that," wrote Casey. "All you had to do to find out whether or not a man had been in the lynching party was to say 'strangler' in front of him. The real stranglers would run up a temperature and fill the air with alibis."

No one who could actually identify the guilty was talking, so there was little for the coroner's jury to do but state the obvious: Louis Curry, A.J. Allen and James Hall, "came to their death

from hanging by the neck with a rope suspended to the limb
of a pine tree near Rapid City, D.T., between the hours of one
and five a.m., June 21st, 1877, by parties to the Jury unknown."

Hall couldn't even escape from his ill-chosen companions in
death. Their bodies were left to dangle until the next day, then
unceremoniously dumped into a common grave marked by a
pine board headstone bearing this epitaph:

HORSE THIEVES BEWARE
Here lies the bodies of Allen, Curry and Hall
Like other thieves, they had their rise, decline and fall.
On yon pine tree they hung till dead
And here they found a lonely bed.
Then be a little cautious how you gobble horses up,
For every horse you pick up here, adds sorrow to your cup;
We're bound to stop this business, or hang you to a man,
For we've hemp and hands enough in town to swing the
*   whole damn clan.*

Robert Casey moved to Rapid City in 1910, more than 33
years after Curry, Allen and Hall died, "but you still could get
yourself thoroughly disliked by discussing the affair," he recalled. "Every now and then . . . when you started to talk with
some pioneer about Rapid City's chances for the prosperity
that seemed about due, he would look all around him like the
third conspirator. And if nobody was looking at him he would
whisper huskily: 'This town won't get nowhere till all them that
took part in the Hangman's Hill business is dead.'"

Some of the "necktie party" were rumored to be prominent
members of the community, and that belief is made more plau-
sible by the heartbreaking ordeal of the lynch mob's fourth and
final victim, a character known simply as Old Man Wright.

Wright tried to talk the vigilantes out of their dastardly business that night, "and for two years afterward he tried to get an
investigation into the case," wrote Fielder. "At last he gained
enough support to bring a grand jury to town. Elated, he rode

through the Hills, begging witnesses to come to Rapid to testify. He offered to pay their expenses. The thing had become an obsession with him, and he was determined to leave no stone unturned."

Old Man Wright hadn't reckoned with the murderers' determination to bury the matter, however. Years after the fact one of the grand jurymen was quoted in a Rapid City newspaper as saying, "all who deemed it inadvisable to have this outrage aired in courts and given out to the world [united] in circulating the report that, in their opinion, old man Wright had become demented and should be removed to the insane asylum in Yankton," wrote McClintock.

Wright was somehow tricked into traveling to Yankton, accompanied by a doctor who was in league with those who wanted to silence him. Once they arrived, the doctor's perjured testimony got Wright committed, "and the old man's heart was broken when he saw how he had been duped," Fielder wrote. "He could take it no longer. He became ill in the asylum shortly afterward and died. The grand jury investigation was forgotten."

And the hangmen went free.

SEE FOR YOURSELF

One of Rapid City's most popular visitors' attractions occupies the site where condemned men were once sent to die. Decades ago spectators solemnly ascended Hangman's Hill, but today children squeal in delight at the life size creatures that comprise Dinosaur Park.

Emmett Sullivan spearheaded the Works Progress Administration's project during the Great Depression. Locals were skeptical; some even called it "Eyesore Park." But the seven green and white dinosaurs have become Black Hills icons. Rapid Citians watched intently in 2012 as the 75-year-old creatures were carefully restored and repainted.

Hangman's Hill is just west of downtown Rapid City, where Skyline Drive makes a sharp corner and follows Dinosaur Park. The park is open daily June through October. Call (605) 343-8687 for information.

CHAPTER 8

Doc Middleton

The Unwickedest Outlaw

DOC MIDDLETON "growed up from a bad seed," as they used to say. His father was either his mother's brother-in-law, who had also fathered her first child when she was 14, or a man named Middleton who got himself hanged for murder the year Doc was born.

On the day of his birth in 1851, Doc was given the name James Middleton Riley — a bequest which he didn't consider binding. He used and discarded at least a dozen aliases over the years, and even got married under a false name, all in a never-ending quest to escape his past and confound the law.

Doc Middleton's life of crime commenced at the tender age of 14 when he stole a horse; he graduated to murder four years later by tracking down and killing a teacher who had defiled his younger sister. That's how it went with Doc. Sometimes he had a "good" reason for the murders he committed. Like the time he beat his first wife's brother to death with a fence rail because the man was abusing his (Doc's) grandmother. Other men were just unlucky to have crossed paths with Doc Middleton. Like the ranch hand he killed in a fight, or the unknown number of men he proudly claimed to have killed while they were trying to apprehend him for his crimes.

Middleton was sent to Huntsville Prison for stealing horses rather than murder, ironically, but it hardly mattered because he escaped nine months later. He fled Texas and eventually

Doc Middleton was a Nebraska outlaw who gravitated northward to run saloons in southwestern South Dakota.

ended up in Sidney, Nebraska, where he shot and killed a soldier in a barroom brawl. Most witnesses held the soldier responsible because he started the fight, but Middleton was nonetheless indicted for murder. He absconded to northern Nebraska, "which at that time was unorganized territory, where bad men roamed at will knowing no law but the six-shooter and the Bowie knife," wrote S.D. Butcher in *Pioneer History of Custer County.*

For a man of Middleton's inclinations, this was paradise. He and his gang ranged across the Niobrara River watershed, up into Dakota Territory and west to Wyoming, stealing anything on four legs. Middleton reportedly stole 3,000 horses and hundreds of cattle in 1877-78, and the rugged, sparsely settled land provided plenty of places to hide the stock until he could work his magic: he had earned the nickname "Doc" because of his skill at doctoring brands to disguise an animal's true ownership.

Middleton never victimized his immediate neighbors unless they antagonized him. He preferred to prey on the Indians, or distant ranches, so the area's white settlers were inclined to look the other way. Doc even earned a reputation as a cowboy Robin Hood by leaving horses he'd stolen elsewhere at the homesteads of poor folk. Every family in the area, seemingly, had a tale of some good deed done by Doc Middleton, which led one writer to dub him "the unwickedest outlaw" in the Black Hills and Niobrara country.

Not everyone shared that attitude, of course. Middleton crossed paths with a vigilante lynch mob and somehow talked his way out of a rope — it was rumored that he had helped one of them out of a financial jam — but his luck eventually ran out and he was captured in a raucous shootout near Laughing Creek. Even though the black-bearded scoundrel shot a U.S. marshal in an escape attempt, he was only sentenced to five years in a Nebraska prison.

After that stint, Middleton gained some respectability. He performed in Buffalo Bill Cody's Wild West Show and was one of nine cowboys who competed in the famous Chadron-to-Chicago horse race in 1893. Doc was considered the favorite because he knew Nebraska's back country so well, but his mounts played out long before he reached Chicago and he finished out of the money.

Stealing horses is a young man's game, so Doc gave it up for the life of a saloonkeeper. That was the business that brought him to Ardmore, South Dakota, just a mile from the state line in south central Fall River County. He settled there in 1903, although "settled" was a relative term for the outlaw. Doc Middleton never murdered anybody while he was in Ardmore, it's true, but he did have to subdue an unruly saloon patron by beating him with a hammer. And there was a dispute over a sack of potatoes that escalated into a street brawl. The potato seller got in the first blow and knocked Doc on his behind, and that indignity was compounded because the pint of whiskey he had in his back pocket broke when he landed.

Doc Middleton was married to his third wife, Rene Richard-

SEE FOR YOURSELF

Doc Middleton is not forgotten in the Sandhills and shortgrass country of northwest Nebraska and southwest South Dakota, and in fact the Black Hills Saloon Company in the little Fall River County town of Oelrichs still serves refreshments and sandwiches on a big, ornate walnut bar that some local folks believe was once owned by the entrepreneurial outlaw. Oelrichs is south of Hot Springs at the junction of Highways 385 and 18.

son, by this time. He had spirited her away from her family's Sandhills ranch when she was only 15, but their union endured longer than his other marriages. They had five children together, and all but one survived to adulthood. "Doc was good to his family and provided well for them," in mostly legal ways, wrote Harold Hutton in *Doc Middleton: Life and Legends of the Notorious Outlaw*. "He might steal coal off a gondola car … but the railroad was considered fair game."

Stealing coal wasn't likely to provide much excitement for a man accustomed to living on the wrong side of the law. When Doc decided he'd had enough of being a respectable citizen he moved on, and found more than he was looking for.

"Doc Middleton … is having plenty of trouble of his own at the present," reported the *Harrison Sun* on the day after Christmas, 1913. "He was arrested and thrown into jail at Douglas, Wyoming, for running a saloon contrary to law, and while in jail, contracted erysipelas, which is going very hard with him. His two sons were sent for, and are with him, and his chances of getting well are not very encouraging. Well, old Doc has seen more fun (such as it was) and excitement in the [62] years he has lived than most men would, should they live to be a thousand years old."

Doc Middleton died in bed on December 27, 1913 of natural causes. That's a luxury he denied his many victims.

CHAPTER 9

Lame Johnny
An Intelligent Horse Thief

THE COVERED WAGON (recognized throughout the Black Hills as a "treasure coach") lumbered southward along the Cheyenne to Deadwood Trail. Its given name was the *Monitor*, a tribute to the first U.S. Navy battleship to be constructed with iron in 1861. In that respect, the Dakota Territory stagecoach and the renowned Civil War ship shared a characteristic. The coach, specially built in Cheyenne four months earlier, was lined with 5/16-inch iron plate to help protect the precious cargo it was assigned to carry. On this day — September 26, 1878 — that amounted to over $27,000 in gold and other valuables from the Homestake Gold Mine in Lead.

Shortly before 3 p.m., a man on horseback sauntered into the Canyon Springs station, about 35 miles south of Deadwood, and asked for water. William Miner, the station attendant, was happy to oblige. But as he fetched the water, the mysterious man quickly dismounted and drew a gun. He bound Miner and locked him inside the granary. Then a group of masked horsemen rode into the station and went inside. They poked their gun barrels through holes in the building's log walls and waited.

At promptly 3 p.m. the *Monitor* pulled into Canyon Springs. When the attendant failed to appear, driver Gene Barnett and his assistant Galen Hill dismounted to find him. As soon as their feet touched the earth, gunfire erupted.

Hill was shot in the left arm. He drew and spun to return

fire when a rifle blast struck him squarely in the chest. A shot through the roof of the coach grazed the head of Captain Eugene Smith, one of the cargo's guards, and knocked him unconscious. The other guard, Scott Davis, opened fire. He and telegraph operator Hugh Campbell, riding to his new job at the Jenney Stockade station in Wyoming, decided to flee the coach and run for cover under a large pine tree. But Campbell was wounded as he ran and fell to the ground, where he was shot and killed.

Barnett tried to whip the six-horse team into a run, but one of the robbers grabbed the reins. Davis shot him as another outlaw emerged and took Barnett hostage. Outnumbered, Davis retreated into the forest. The rest of the gang dragged the *Monitor* into the trees and transferred its treasure into their own wagon. When they finished two hours later, they tied Barnett and Smith to the *Monitor*'s wheels and rode southwest into the deep canyons of the Southern Black Hills.

Relief messengers Boone May, Bill Sample and Jesse Brown awaited the *Monitor* at the Beaver Creek station, farther south on the trail. When it didn't arrive, they mounted horses and rode toward Canyon Springs. They met Davis furiously riding south for help. They all returned to the site of the robbery, where they found the looted *Monitor* and Miner still locked in the granary.

Stories of stagecoach robberies and other exciting tales from the Old West are rarely complete because important details disappeared into history. This story is no different, but there are two established facts: the *Monitor* was robbed, and two of the three gold ingots stolen that day remain missing. What we don't know is whether one of the grandest stagecoach robberies in Black Hills history was orchestrated by a handicapped horse thief named Lame Johnny, who terrorized the Hills for three years before he was mysteriously hanged from an old elm tree.

The West was filled with outlaws who turned to crime as a last resort for survival because their skills presented no other opportunities. Not so with Lame Johnny, who was born Cornelius Donahue in Philadelphia in 1854. At age 8 he was admitted to the city's Stephen Girard College where he graduated near the top of his class in 1872 with a grade point average of 9.8 out of a possible 10. The lure of the Wild West brought him to Texas, where he tried ranch work and learned the art of horse thievery. Apache Indians frequently stole large herds of ranch horses. Texas cowboys showed Donahue the finer points of stealing them back.

Perhaps drawn by the gold rush, Donahue appeared in the Black Hills in the spring of 1876. He met John Francis Murphy, who was freighting goods from Cheyenne to Deadwood. Donahue introduced himself as John Hurley and asked for a job. Murphy gave him a horse and put him to work.

Hurley reportedly served briefly as a deputy sheriff in Custer County. He also worked as a bookkeeper at Homestake until a Texan recognized him as Donahue the horse thief.

That's apparently when Hurley turned to a full time life of crime and gained the moniker Lame Johnny. One of his feet was badly deformed, but explanations behind the malady differ. Some accounts say he suffered from polio as a child. Another says he fell off a horse. Still another claims he was shot in the leg while in Texas. His telltale limp made him widely recognizable and led to unique problems. One foot was two sizes smaller than the other, so boot makers always requested a deposit. They figured the shoes would never sell if Johnny didn't collect them.

Lame Johnny was best at stealing horses, so that's what he did. He was prospecting along Castle Creek during the summer of 1876 when a band of Indians stole his horses. Johnny borrowed a friend's horse, rode to the Red Cloud Agency, killed the corral guard and drove 300 horses to the Black Hills.

Black Hills residents marveled at how Lame Johnny could steal huge herds of horses, and then simply disappear with them in the Hills. In March 1879, he and partners Tony Pastor and a man named "Brocky" herded 68 head of stock on the Pine Ridge Reservation and headed toward the Southern Hills. A band of Indians pursued them and shot Brocky in the arm. The trio was caught in a fierce spring blizzard before they reached the Hills, and they soon became lost. Johnny and Pastor found shelter, but they lost Brocky in the storm. He was never seen again.

At some point horse thievery became a gateway to robbing stagecoaches. Outlaw Frank Harris testified in court that he, Lame Johnny and Tom Moore robbed a coach on January 9, 1879 as it crossed Dry Creek, six miles from Buffalo Gap. "I stopped the coach," Harris recalled. "Tom Moore went through passengers. Lame Johnny stood on the side opposite me and made the passengers throw up their hands."

Harris reported they took two silver watches, one gold watch and $10 to $15 in cash. Lame Johnny stole a batch of 2-cent stamps. They also searched sacks of mail, but found nothing valuable.

Lame Johnny and Harris were finally captured in 1879 on the Pine Ridge Reservation. They were held at Fort Robinson, Nebraska, until July 1, when Johnny was turned over to James "Whispering" Smith, a noted railroad detective who had been stationed in Sidney to help capture Deadwood stagecoach robbers.

The two traveled to Red Cloud station, north of the fort, to meet a stagecoach bound for Deadwood, where Johnny would stand trial. He was shackled, and a blacksmith fashioned leg irons attached to a metal plate, which was then bolted to the floor of the carriage. Ed Cook, a driver whom Johnny had once robbed, drove the stage. Smith rode next to him. Shotgun messenger Jesse Brown, with his wife and two daughters, rode inside. Legendary treasure coach guard and shotgun messenger Boone May accompanied as an outrider.

Trees and hills became shadows against the moonlit sky as the stagecoach rolled north. The party was 8 miles north of Buffalo Gap when, at about 11 p.m., a cadre of as many as eight masked men stopped them. They pried the metal plate from the coach floor and dragged Johnny into the brush. Some accounts say they demanded Johnny disclose the names of his gang members and to confess his crimes. When Johnny refused, they said they planned to hang him. "Hang and be damned," Johnny is said to have replied. "You can't do it any too soon."

The men promptly escorted Johnny to a nearby elm tree and hanged him. They retreated through the Hills, and the coach that had transported Johnny continued on its way. Historians have noted with curiosity that none of Johnny's guards, including the sharpshooting Boone May, expended much effort to protect their prisoner.

Members of Pete Oslund's freighting crew found Lame Johnny's body the following day. They buried him, shackles and all, on the spot. Not long after Johnny's death, a group of men from Deadwood visited the grave to investigate the means by which he died. Rumors had spread that Johnny had been shot before he was hanged. When they exhumed his corpse, they were shocked to discover the head was missing. Legend says hired guns like Boone May sometimes decapitated their victims in order to claim rewards, but no proof surfaced. They removed Johnny's shackles and reburied him in his original grave. Somebody constructed a crude wooden headboard that marked the gravesite for years. It read:

Pilgrim Pause!
You're standing on
The molding clay of Limping John
Tread lightly, stranger, on this sod,
For if he moves, you're robbed, by God.

The *Black Hills Times* announced Lame Johnny's fate to its readers on July 3. "It is altogether probable that Lame Johnny, a road agent, horse thief and a bad man on general principles, has gone up to push clouds against the sun," it reported. The story recounted his abduction from the stagecoach and figured his chances of survival were "about equal to a thousand to nothing."

Thus ended the life of one of the Black Hills' most notorious outlaws. But what about the infamous *Monitor* robbery from the fall of 1878? Soon after the heist, Luke Voorhees, superintendent of the Cheyenne and Black Hills Stage Company, offered a $2,500 reward for the capture of the outlaws and the safe return of the cargo, which in addition to the three gold ingots included 1,056 ounces of gold dust and nuggets, $500 in diamonds, $500 in jewelry and $2,000 in currency. The Homestake mine also reportedly offered its own reward. The federal government extended a bounty of $200 per robber, and Dakota Territory Gov. William Howard put forth $1,000. With serious money on the table, numerous posses, led by intimidating figures like Boone May and Seth Bullock, set out on the gang's trail.

Within days, the robbers began making mistakes. In October Archie McLaughlin and Bill Mansfield tried to sell some of the pilfered gold in Deadwood. They were arrested and sent to Cheyenne for trial. The men went through numerous trial delays and were frequently shipped between Cheyenne and Deadwood. One day during transport, a group of vigilantes stopped the coach and hanged the accused from two huge cottonwood trees.

Charles Carey, the gang's alleged ringleader, had doubled back during his escape and was caught near the site of the robbery. He was hanged at Jenney Stockade in Wyoming on October 3. Frank McBride, the outlaw shot as he tried to wrangle

SEE FOR YOURSELF

One of the shackles that confined Lame Johnny during his final stagecoach ride is housed at the museum of the South Dakota State Historical Society in Pierre. Call (605) 773-3458. The other, along with a piece of the elm tree from which he was hanged, is displayed at the 1881 Courthouse Museum in Custer. Call (605) 673-2443.

the horses from the *Monitor's* driver Barnett, died from his wounds and was buried as the gang fled through the Hills.

Within six weeks of the robbery, roughly 60 percent of the stolen loot was recovered. Nearly a dozen men were eventually arrested and charged with some degree of participation in the Canyon Springs heist. The only unknowns were the location of the two gold ingots and if Lame Johnny had been involved. Following a stagecoach robbery on October 2, 1877 in which one of the passengers recognized Lame Johnny, no one with his trademark limp was reported to be involved in any stage-coach crimes. Survivors of the *Monitor* robbery would have noticed a limping bandit. Some scholars of the West maintain that Johnny never associated with Carey's gang, while others are confident that he somehow played a role.

Despite his stage heists, Lame Johnny's status as one of the Hills' slickest horse thieves survived for nearly 100 years. But in the 1960s, the secret to his success may have been revealed. When Johnny and his gang stole horses, they rode toward Buffalo Gap and disappeared into the canyons near King's Ridge. Orval Halstead filed a homestead claim on King's Ridge in 1919. One snowy morning, he discovered a steer missing from his herd. Halstead followed its tracks to the rim of a box canyon and found the steer, far below on the canyon floor, seemingly uninjured. Halstead investigated and found an old trail obscured by three large rocks that led to two hidden caves. Inside he discovered a corral that could hold as many as 30 horses. The other cave was strewn with rotten ropes, bottles, cans, boots and bedding. The family believed they had discovered the remains of Lame Johnny's hideout.

Of course no one can prove Lame Johnny was ever there, just as no one can prove he robbed the *Monitor*. The only sure thing about Lame Johnny is that there will always be more questions than answers.

CHAPTER 10

Fools for Gold

Miners, Swindlers and Hoaxers

ANCIENT GREEKS saw gold as a treat for the immortal gods, but the rowdy miners that sought it in the streams and hillsides of Dakota Territory were mere mortals. The immediate demand for mountain cemeteries was proof of that.

One trait the miners shared was a lust for riches. Black Elk, a leader of the Lakota Sioux, referred to gold as the yellow mineral "that drives the white man crazy."

The Black Hills Gold Rush officially began on August 2, 1874 when two prospectors with the Custer Expedition found nuggets in French Creek. Word could not have spread more quickly — not even if the Internet had existed back then. Hordes of trespassing miners were soon in the Black Hills of Dakota Territory. All were optimistic that they'd soon be rich.

Professor Walter Jenney reportedly plucked a rosebush in 1876 below Harney Peak and found gold dust clinging to its petals. The town of Hayward was instantly created to serve the 300 miners who arrived with pick axes and sluice boxes.

Gold from Hayward and other mining camps was sent away on well-guarded stagecoaches, but robbers had followed the miners. Custer County historian Martha Linde wrote that the Harney Stage was especially vulnerable because the road to Hayward had dense, pine-thick canyons that provided cover for an ambush.

"The early stage drivers were much-admired, skillful, brave

and friendly men," wrote Linde in *Rushmore's Golden Valleys.*

A writer by the name of J.W. Buel witnessed the mayhem of the mining camps and wrote a book in 1886 in which he described the Black Hills' roughest place as follows:

Deadwood, like every other big mining town that has yet been located in the West, was full of rough characters, cut-throats, gamblers and the devil's agents generally. Night and day the wild orgies of depraved humanity continued; a fiddler was an important personage, provided he would hire out to saw all night in a saloon, and the concert singer was a bo-nanza, especially if the voice were clothed in petticoats. The arbiter of all disputes was either a knife or pistol, and the graveyard soon started with a steady run of victims. Sodom and Gomorrah were both dull, stupid towns compared with Deadwood, for in a square contest for the honors of moral depravity the Black Hills capital could have given the people of the Dead Sea cities three points in the game and then skunk them both.

Still, silver-tongued salesmen were more likely to steal fortunes than common bandits. Sweet-talking mine promoters found it easy to attract Easterners with money who were en-amored with the western notion that there was gold to be had — on rose petals, even? — and eager to get their share without even getting their hands dirtied or callused.

In some instances, the promoters were respected citizens. Tom Sweeney, one of Rapid City's founding fathers, faked a placer gold discovery in Rapid Creek to attract miners from the Northern Hills who were becoming discouraged as the easy deposits played out around Deadwood.

Big Hat Clark, who once performed with Buffalo Bill Cody's Wild West Show, was among the best at selling op-portunity. "He was a familiar sight in Keystone," wrote Linde, "with his big black western hat, wearing his buffalo coat from the Pony Express days and riding his large white horse. He was a handsome man with well-trimmed, bushy eyebrows and long, black wavy hair kept nicely shaped. He was a man with

NAME YOUR MINE

Gold mining is a relatively rare pastime in the Black Hills today, but you can still file for a claim, which gives you permission to dig or pan on about 20 acres in the Black Hills National Forest. Call the Black Hills National Forest (605-673-9200) for maps and details.

You'll want to name your mine. Historically, mines have been named for famous characters, interesting geography, intriguing women, or heartfelt feelings. You might find inspiration in these all-time favorite names:

- Holy Terror Mine, named after the miner's wife

- Homestake, derived from the miners' hopes of getting a stake to buy a home

- Balky Mule Mine, on Jim Creek in Pennington County, for an obvious reason

- Bengal Tiger Mine, northwest of Hill City, for black and yellow streaks of ore

- Black Nell Mine in honor of a madam from Deadwood

- Yankee Boy Mine in Lawrence County, named by William Fagen for his favorite chewing tobacco

- Antietam Mine, claimed by David Ellis, who fought in the Civil War's famous Battle of Antietam

Once gold was discovered deep within a Black Hills mountain, water was used to flush any nuggets or tiny flakes toward miners waiting downstream.

a magnetic personality and when he went East on numerous trips for financial backing, his friends had great confidence in his ability."

Clark and other mine owners and promoters may have had good intentions, but the investors' money and patience were almost always exhausted before any significant amounts of gold, silver or tin were discovered.

"Mining and fraud have long been synonymous," wrote Spearfish historian David A. Wolff in a 2003 article for *South Dakota History.* "Unscrupulous men promising great fortunes have tried to separate the unwise from their money. Mark Twain once described a mine as a 'hole in the ground owned by a liar.'"

Twain and Black Elk must have met Robert Flormann, who came to the Black Hills in 1876 intent on striking it rich in the gold rush. He bought claims along Box Elder Creek and spread rumors that his land contained more gold than the Homestake Mine near Lead.

Newspapers in Chicago reported Flormann's find, which he named the Greenwood Mine. But he needed investors, so he convinced Joseph Taylor, a prominent English mineralogist, to legitimize his operation. Taylor knew immediately that the Greenwood Mine wasn't worth the train ticket that brought him West. But he shared Flormann's ambition, and they agreed to work together to promote the mine. Taylor traveled to Chicago, where he successfully baited Matthew Laflin. When Laflin visited the Hills to take ore samples, Flormann and Taylor al-

SEE FOR YOURSELF

Olaf Seim and James Nelson started the Broken Boot Mine near Deadwood in 1878. They never found real gold, but they did discover a good vein of fool's gold, which was the next best thing. Fool's gold is rich in iron pyrite, which produces sulfuric acid, a chemical necessary in mining camps for processing gold ore.

Thanks to that, Seim and Nelson kept the mine going until 1904. It reopened during WWI for a few years, and then closed again until 1954, when Seim's daughter aired out the old tunnels and started a tourist attraction. Today a non-profit group provides tours, and kids are invited to pan for gold in a sluice. They always go away with a flake or two of real gold.

Call (605) 578-1876 for more information on the Broken Boot, or dig into www.brokenbootmine.com.

legedly switched his bag with another containing richer pieces. Laflin, convinced that uncountable wealth lay beneath his feet, contributed $100,000.

The Greenwood Gold Mining and Milling Company operated until January, 1885, when investors noticed something amiss. After processing 3,000 tons of ore, just $5 worth of gold had been extracted. The mine closed, but Laflin lost some $300,000 in total. One wag joked that the only gold in Greenwood "was in Professor Taylor's teeth."

All the gold-digging swindlers were not in the Black Hills. George Henry came up empty handed in Colorado, so he moved to the Oakwood Lakes area in eastern South Dakota and in the fall of 1883 claimed to have found gold there. Some believed it was a hoax, but the adage "find it and they will come" held true. Miners, farmers and townspeople by the hundreds flocked to the lake hoping to strike it rich, according to Chuck Cecil who wrote about the episode in his Brookings County history, *Fire the Anvils, Beat the Drums*.

"Henry said the nuggets he found ranged from the size of

SEE FOR YOURSELF

Visit the Adams Museum in Deadwood where, among many other things, you can see Potato Creek Johnny's gigantic 7.75-ounce gold nugget. Is it the largest ever found in the Black Hills — or did he fuse several together? The closest competitor to Johnny's is the Ice Box Nugget, which was discovered just a few years ago by modern-day prospector Charlie "Digger" Ward. His 5.27-ouncer now resides at the Clock Shop in downtown Rapid City.

the head of a pin to as big as a kernel of wheat," wrote Cecil. "His brother, William J. Henry, came from Wisconsin to lend him a hand. William was also a miner and a geologist. The two men and Robert Henry went to work looking out for their bonanza on the northwest point of East Oakwood Lake. Others followed suit. Men were everywhere along the lake shore. Some set up a derrick on the school section near the lake and dug deep searching for the gold that was never found."

The Brookings County miners had only slightly less luck than most of their Black Hills contemporaries.

Pirates and thieves had codes of honor, and so did most of the miners. Martha Linde, the Custer author, said there was a Ninth Commandment that read as follows: "Thou shalt not tell any false tales about gold diggin's in the mountains to thy neighbor, that thou may benefit a friend who has mules, provisions, tools and blankets that he cannot sell, lest in deceiving thy neighbor, when he returneth through the snow with naught save his rifle, he presents thee with the contents thereof and like a dog shall fall down and die."

That readeth like the golden rule.

Stories of Poker Alice may contradict one another, but photos of her puffing on a cigar with a glowering expression fix her place in history books.

CHAPTER 11

Poker Alice

A Cigar-smoking Contradiction

IT'S HARD TO BELIEVE, looking at her dour portraits with those omnipresent cigars, but Poker Alice Tubbs is the only South Dakotan ever portrayed by Elizabeth Taylor.

On the other hand, she was played by a chicken at Bewitched Village, a trained animal act at Reptile Gardens west of Rapid City. That's Poker Alice for you. Long after her death, her legend retains remarkable staying power, whether interpreted by Hollywood royalty or Rapid City poultry.

But what parts of that legend are to be believed? Is she most accurately remembered as a brothel madam or a professional gambler? A hard-working homesteader, a quick-trigger killer, a Sunday school teacher, a Sturgis political power, or a local embarrassment? The stories contradict one another at every turn.

A granite headstone in St. Aloysius Cemetery above Sturgis records her birth as 1851, though some historians say 1853. It's mostly agreed she entered this world in England and never lost her British accent, but there's census data listing Virginia as her birth place. Did she move to Louisiana as a child with her family? Did her father fight for the Confederacy during the Civil War? Did she enroll in a fine southern finishing school? Depends on whom you want to believe.

Was she, as some western writers insist, a stunning beauty in her youth? That might be a stretch, judging by early portraits.

But she turned the head of one Frank Duffield, probably while still in her teens, and the couple briefly enjoyed married life in a Colorado mining camp, until Frank died in a mine explosion. The accident happened in the early 1870s, and some Poker Alice promoters worked hard to establish her presence in the Black Hills during or shortly after the 1876 gold rush.

Not likely. But half a century after the gold rush, Poker Alice was an available personality as Deadwood marketed itself at railroad and newspaper-sponsored travel shows, and when the community staged its first Days of '76 celebrations. Alice's Sturgis brothel had just been busted, and it's likely she appreciated any amenities her promotional appearances generated, even if nothing more than a free dinner.

Promoters have always wanted to have Alice in the Black Hills as early as possible, but there is no credible evidence that she was there in the 1870s or '80s. Three years before her 1930 death, Alice told writer Courtney Ryley Cooper about residing and gambling in Colorado during the 1880s, and being a part of Creede, Colorado's silver boom in the early 1890s. She more than likely moved to South Dakota after that.

Poker Alice dealt cards in several states before setting up shop in South Dakota.

Alice married again, this time to Warren Tubbs in 1892, according to Tubbs' 1910 obituary. Did the couple have children? Seven, say some sources. None, say others — after all, Alice was about 40 when they married. And then there's a story that Alice had a daughter, by Tubbs or before Tubbs, and turned her over to the Benedictine sisters who founded Sturgis' St. Martin's Academy. The sisters came to the Black Hills from Switzerland and, the story goes, shipped the child to Switzerland where she grew up not knowing her mother's identity. The plot smacks of Victorian-era fiction, and folks familiar with Black Hills history have heard a nearly identical tale told of Calamity Jane.

There's evidence that Alice and Warren Tubbs were in the Black Hills, not looking for gold, card games, or infamy, but hoping to succeed in agriculture. They eventually lived on a homestead north of Sturgis, and Warren made money painting houses in town. He developed respiratory trouble, perhaps caused or worsened by paint fumes, and died on the homestead during a heavy snow, the last day of 1909. Alice apparently let the body freeze, knowing it would be awhile before she could drive a wagon through snow drifts to the undertaker.

Maybe Alice had dealt poker hands before — in Colorado, Oklahoma, New Mexico, and Arizona. Those states all claim stories about her, including a dubious one that had her dealing cards for saloon-keeper Bob Ford, who killed Jesse James. But as far as the Black Hills go, Alice probably became Poker Alice only after Warren died.

Nearly 60, she set up shop in a two-story clapboard house a few blocks off Sturgis' Main Street, near Bear Butte Creek. Her main customers were lonely Fort Meade soldiers, and her goods and services were liquor, poker games and prostitutes. Her house was also known for its flowers and angora cats. Contrary to a popular Black Hills myth, the pets did not inspire the slang expression "cat house," in use before Alice went into business.

George Moses, the late Black Hills tailor and amateur historian, recalled that anyone Poker Alice knew could buy a drink anytime — after the bars in Deadwood closed at 2 a.m., and after Prohibition became law in 1920. "In all the years I knew Poker Alice, I never saw her in a dress," Moses wrote in his book, *Those Good Old Days in the Black Hills*. "She always dressed in an army shirt, trousers, and a man's hat. She always had a cigar in her mouth."

There are naive stories told about brothel madams everywhere, and in the Black Hills they've all been adapted for

Poker Alice; no one matched her charitable giving; she wielded great political power because she had so much money and knew so many secrets; she led her girls in weekly Sunday school lessons.

A glance through Sturgis newspapers of the era suggests a harsher reality. Poker Alice regularly knew legal troubles, and politicians won votes promising to shut down her house. Her darkest misadventure resulted in a cavalry sergeant's death and injuries to a private. Their group of cavalrymen arrived at the house one night only to discover it full of patrons. The latecomers, writes Bob Lee in *Fort Meade and the Black Hills,* "vented their frustration by cutting telephone and power lines to the house and pelting the house with rocks. A number of

Bernie Hunhoff

SEE FOR YOURSELF

Visit or stay in Poker Alice's tidy white house with green trim on Junction Avenue in Sturgis. The home, built in 1895, once featured a poker room, gambling and dance halls and brothel in addition to Poker Alice's living quarters. Today her house has five bedrooms, private and shared baths and can accommodate 10 people. Call the Star Lite Motel at (605) 347-2506 for information.

shots were fired, and when the smoke cleared, the two soldiers were down with bullet wounds." Sturgis residents generally believed Poker Alice herself pulled the trigger, but she wasn't charged for assault because she was acting in self defense. She was, however, fined for running a brothel.

During her years as a Sturgis madam, Poker Alice married a third husband, George Huckert, but he soon died. While there were rumors of an unhappy fourth marriage, the main man in Alice's life by the 1920s was a tough nemesis — Jack Everett. When he became state's attorney, he aggressively went after her business, not only as a place of prostitution, but for violating new Prohibition laws. Everett successfully prosecuted, had the house closed, and got Poker Alice sentenced to prison. But Gov. William Bulow kept Alice free with a pardon, supposedly saying he, "couldn't send a white-haired lady to prison."

Alice was just shy of her 78th birthday when the pardon came in November, 1928. A photographer arranged to take a picture of the occasion, but no one in the photo looks remotely happy — not the official who hand-delivered the pardon, and not Alice. Perhaps the whole Poker Alice experience had grown entirely stale, both for Sturgis and for the woman herself. She died 15 months later.

And with her passing, she really became Poker Alice. Her scowling face appears on postcards available in every Black Hills gift shop. She is a feature of every Black Hills history book written after her death, fact and fiction blurring more with each passing decade. She is still a presence at Days of '76 each August, lovingly portrayed by cigar-chomping imitators.

Elizabeth Taylor's portrayal came in 1987, in a CBS TV movie titled "Poker Alice." As if there weren't enough Poker Alice stories from which to choose, script writers invented a new one: Alice wins the brothel in a card game. The movie found a fresh look for its subject, too — blue satin, lots of lace, and a dainty parasol. The role appealed to Taylor, she told a newspaper writer, because, "I have been a gambler all my life. I think I've gambled with life."

The role did little to enhance Taylor's own legend. The movie, shot in Arizona, attracted scant attention except in the Black Hills. Filming coincided with discussions in Sturgis about preserving Poker Alice's house, fallen into disrepair, nearly wiped away in the 1972 Black Hills flood and considered an eyesore by many residents.

Jim Quinn, then director of the town's chamber of commerce, offered Taylor an expense-paid Black Hills trip if she'd kick off a fund-raising campaign to preserve Alice's house. Gov. George Mickelson liked the idea and added his own invitation. In his letter to the movie star, the governor related his favorite Poker Alice story, about how she paid off a bank loan early. How, wondered her banker, did she come up with the money so fast?

"Well, it's this way," Alice replied in Mickelson's story. "I'd knowed that the Grand Army of the Republic was a-goin' to have its encampment here in Sturgis — I knowed about that. And I'd knowed that the state Elks' convention would be here, too. But you know, I plumb forgot about the Methodist District Conference!"

Through her publicist, Taylor replied that her schedule wouldn't permit a Black Hills visit, adding that her charitable giving was directed toward AIDS research. But shortly the house project found a benefactor close to home. Sturgis motel owner Ted Walker bought the building from the city for a dollar, moved it onto a lot next to his motel on Junction Avenue, and put up the money to refurbish the old home, which today he rents to guests. Not surprisingly, the house came with its own set of stories, some involving ghosts.

— *By Paul Higbee*

CHAPTER 12

Jack Sully

Rosebud Rogue or Robin Hood?

JACK SULLY LAY BLEEDING on a Gregory County hillside. Tall prairie grass waved in the breeze around him as he gazed into the vast South Dakota sky. Slowly he extended his arm to U.S. Marshal John Petrie, who knelt beside him. The two men were allies once, but on the morning of May 16, 1904, Petrie had led the posse that chased Sully from his home in the Rosebud country. The two shook hands. And then Sully, one of the West's most polarizing figures, died.

Jack Sully is respected or reviled, depending on whom you ask. He's either an upstanding lawman and friendly rancher who never shied from helping downtrodden families, or the mastermind of an extensive cattle-rustling network that operated for decades across the Upper Midwest and Canada. Perhaps he was both.

Sully was born in Ireland in 1839, just six years before the Great Potato Famine and drought swept across the country. Nearly one million people died or left Ireland between 1845 and 1852, and the Sullys were no different. Sully's mother died when he was young. His father, Thomas, gathered his six children, boarded the *Olive Branch* in 1850 and sailed for America. The family arrived in Massachusetts and eventually settled in Chicago. When Sully was 16 he traveled to Minneapolis and became a messenger at Fort Snelling. He was 21 when he chose to fight with the Union during the Civil War, serving with Company K of the 1st Minnesota Infantry.

After the war Sully moved west into Dakota Territory. He became a Pony Express rider, traveling from Yankton to Fort Laramie, Wyoming. When telegraph lines replaced the ponies, Sully worked as a passenger coach driver. He regularly traversed southern Dakota from Yankton to Philip, across rolling river hills and flatlands that would one day bear his name, and into the Black Hills and Wyoming.

During his sojourns through Charles Mix County, he became friends with Cuthbert DuCharme, a trader who ran a roadhouse and represented what passed for law in that part of the territory. When Sully helped apprehend and hang one of DuCharme's rivals for — of all things — cattle rustling in 1872, the citizens of Charles Mix County elected Sully sheriff by a vote of 61-1. The Irishman's margin of victory is even more impressive considering there were only 55 eligible voters.

Residents hoped Sully could curb the violence stemming from competition between Eastern cattle companies, who brought livestock to graze in Dakota's unspoiled grasslands, and the homesteaders that they were methodically squeezing out. Cattle and horse thievery abounded, and settlers fought each other over land.

Jack Sully was a lawman who created one of the largest cattle rustling networks in the Upper Midwest.

Sully's law enforcement career lasted until 1875. Conditions in Charles Mix County had grown so grave that President Ulysses S. Grant closed the area to homesteading, hoping to restore order. It also put Sully out of a job.

He may have sought comfort in the fact that he was soon to be a family man. Jack and Louise Sully were expecting their first child in 1875. After exchanging wedding vows, the Sullys lived along Platte Creek, then moved to Hamilton Island, eventually renamed

Sully Island, where they hoped to raise a family. But Louise and the couple's baby both died during childbirth.

In 1880 Sully married Mary Goulette Kincaid, who was part French, part Lakota and the niece of his first wife. They eventually moved across the river and settled in Gregory County, still part of the Rosebud Indian Reservation, where they raised eight children. There, Sully ran cattle and horses on the plains that came to be called Sully Flats. From Sully's home southwest of Lucas, the flats extended north and east to the Missouri River and south to Whetstone Creek.

By most accounts Sully was well liked. Neighbors said he loved music and dances, was a doting father and often led local Fourth of July parades on horseback. Stories of his good deeds abound. He bought groceries for families too poor to pay. When a young boy new to West River became lost, Sully showed him the trail home. "Now you can go back and tell the folks you just met Jack Sully," he told the wanderer.

But the one-time sheriff had little respect for the law. In 1886 he sold the timber rights on a nearby island to a group of men who immediately began harvesting trees. Since the island was actually part of the Indian reservation, the men were arrested, charged with theft and trespassing and hauled to jail. Locals were ready to take up arms over the conflict until Sully stepped in and diffused the tense situation.

Yet there was another side to Jack Sully. During his years on the Rosebud, he was also the architect of the Circle Society, a ring involving 300 men who stole thousands of cattle from Kansas to Canada. The crew apparently operated for decades by utilizing finely honed methods for stealing cattle. They nabbed only a few head at a time, then laundered the cattle through countless owners until true ownership was impossible to prove.

Sully's huge, L-shaped house stood like a fortress atop a hill, so he could spot lawmen miles away. The second story of his home had one room with no windows and a door that opened directly outside with a ladder to the ground where a horse could be waiting. Some said he built an extensive network of tunnels and well-stocked caves in case he needed a quick getaway.

Sully's exploits led to creative escapes. One time, as a posse pursued him through a driving blizzard, he tunneled into a snowdrift and hid as the lawmen rode past. On another occasion, Sully — again fleeing from a posse — donned female clothing and sat between two women traveling by wagon. The posse stopped the wagon and asked if anyone had seen the outlaw. All three passengers said no, and the groups went their separate ways.

On another occasion, Sully was almost caught branding another man's cattle near Red Rock along the Missouri River. He bolted for the river and rode a floating log all the way to Snake Creek, near today's Platte/Winner bridge.

Few doubt that Sully was a cattle thief, but his motives are debated 100 years later. Some residents of Gregory County still believe Sully was a modern day Robin Hood, stealing from wealthy cattle companies to benefit his poorer neighbors. Between 1866 and 1890, more than 5 million cattle were driven to the open ranges of western Kansas, Nebraska, Wyoming, Montana and the Dakotas to fatten on the abundant grass.

"The big ranchers were pasturing cattle right on top of people," said Jack Broome, a Gregory County historian and retired superintendent of the Burke School District. "People were mad at the big ranchers, and it didn't bother them to steal cattle. In fact, they didn't look on it as stealing. They were basically just defending their land against these big outfits."

Broome's great grandfather, James McMullen, squatted in Gregory County in 1887 north of Bonesteel near Starcher, a tiny village that now lies beneath Lake Francis Case. McMullen once noticed a few head of cattle missing from his herd and accused Sully of taking them. Sully went to McMullen's home. "Jim, you know better than that," Sully told him. "I don't steal from poor people. I steal from rich people."

"A short time later, the cattle that were gone ended up back in my grandfather's pen," Broome said. "Sully knew who took them."

Some of Sully's contemporaries suggested that he was actually an undercover agent, working with the government to apprehend real rustlers, and that made him a target. Joe Ellis, a Sully family friend who ranched near Lake Andes, hinted that might have been true. "Jack was not a bad fellow," Ellis recalled years later. "There were worse men in the country than him, but they were lucky enough to escape the law. They persecuted Jack, and because of spite, never left him alone. He was a good fighter, a game fellow, and a better friend no one ever had, as long as he was treated on the square."

Sully eluded arrest for nearly 30 years. One afternoon in the summer of 1902, he and his son-in-law Joe Blackbird were riding along the Missouri River when they encountered neighbors Harry Ham and Olaf Finstad branding cattle. The animals had been stolen, and when law enforcement discovered the theft, one of the men testified that Sully was responsible. He was arrested during a poker game in Verdigre, Neb., and jailed in Mitchell.

News of Sully's arrest spread quickly. Friends, enemies and curious citizens traveled to Mitchell to see if it was true. They found Sully in good spirits. With a wink, he often told his visitors, "Well, I rustled myself into jail. I reckon I'll just have to rustle myself out."

On January 25, 1903, a deputy went to get Sully's dinner. When he returned, the cell was empty. The padlock on the outer door had been sawed and a lock inside was picked. Sully fled to Joe Ellis' farm, where he stayed overnight. The following morning, he mounted a fresh horse, fled to Canada and disappeared.

The man responsible for capturing Sully was Deputy U.S. Marshal John Petrie. Petrie and Sully were friends who had met during the Civil War. When Sully was Charles Mix County sheriff, he was sometimes spotted in Yankton helping Petrie on various cases.

Now Petrie made it his personal mission to find Sully. He made numerous visits to Sully's farm until Mary Sully finally convinced the lawman that her husband was gone. "The old man simply got tired of being hunted," Petrie told reporters.

No one saw or heard from Jack Sully for over a year. Then in the spring of 1904, the Schilling and Montgomery Cattle Company reported 72 head of cattle missing. A man matching Sully's description was reported to have delivered them in Naper, Neb.

In Chamberlain Petrie and four locals assembled a posse. On the evening of May 15, the group rode into Ben Diamond's ranch, just three miles from Sully's home. The posse convinced Diamond to join them, and they set out a few hours before sunrise.

Accounts differ as to what happened next. One story says Sully was home with his daughter Eva and sons George and John when Diamond rode up to the house on the morning of May 16. Diamond told Sully that the posse would be at his home by noon. Sully continued with farm chores and errands and encountered the mounted group among the hills surrounding his ranch.

A more heroic, bravado-laden account says the posse surrounded Sully while he enjoyed a pancake breakfast with his family. Diamond urged him to surrender. "With fair play, I'm the equal of three of them," Sully said, gently tapping his .44-caliber Colt. Then he raced to the barn and spurred his horse across the prairie.

SEE FOR YOURSELF

Few artifacts of Jack Sully's life remain, but you can pay your respects at the Rosebud rogue's gravesite. The tiny Sully Cemetery is just southwest of Lucas. Find a local historian to guide the way.

Both stories agree that it was likely Deputy Harry Ham who fired the fatal bullet that struck Sully in the back. He tried crawling up a hill but his strength soon left him. He turned over to face his captors. He raised his arm to Petrie, who took his hand and shook it before Sully died. He was 65 years old.

In reporting his death, the *New York Times* called Sully "a lawless and desperate character," "the terror of the Rosebud country," and "the head of a band of rustlers that has been the cause of endless trouble." Mourners converged on Sully's home. A photographer came to document the funeral. One surviving image shows Sully's 9-year-old son Claude holding Jim, the horse his father was riding when he was killed. Another shows Jack Sully lying in an open coffin. He was buried on May 20 in a small family cemetery near his home.

Sully's life soon grew into legend. Sioux Falls writer William Lillibridge is said to have modeled his 1905 book *Ben Blair, The Story of a Plainsman*, upon Sully's life. Virgil and Kate Boyles, a sibling writing team from Yankton, used Sully as inspiration for the main character in their novel *Langford of the Three Bars*, published in 1907.

After that, Sully slowly faded into history. Even his gravesite, marked only with an old wooden post, fell into disrepair. "From the 1930s to probably the 1980s, it was just ignored completely," says Broome, the Gregory County historian. "It was just a little hump out there."

The cemetery holds Sully and three family members. Through decades of neglect, the tiny graveyard became an island in a sea of soybeans and cornfields. In the 1980s, when the landowner threatened to plow the grounds and plant corn, Broome and the local historical society got involved. They built a chain link fence around the cemetery and, citing his service in the Civil War, secured a government issue, white marble stone for Sully's grave.

Since then, there has been renewed interest in the rogue from the Rosebud. His six-shooter with mother-of-pearl grips fetched $18,000 at a Deadwood auction in 2010. And a year

Jack Sully and his wife raised eight children on their Rosebud ranch including Claude, (above) holding his father's horse the day after Sully was killed.

later, Rapid City songwriter Ryan Kickland poignantly wrote about the outlaw's last day in his popular song "The Death of Jack Sully."

Opinions on Jack Sully vary as widely today as they did 100 years ago. We may never know if he was a local Robin Hood, a government agent or an outright thief. We do know he wasn't the only homesteader whose contempt for big business led to rebellious behavior. "I do not look back on my younger days as living the life of a criminal," Sully's neighbor Olaf Finstad wrote years later, "but as one who took part in a battle to protect our right to live."

Maybe if we could ask Jack Sully, he'd say the same thing.

CHAPTER 13

Entrepreneurs & Wool Pullers

SETH BULLOCK is well known to South Dakotans as an early-day horse trader and Deadwood marshal. He was also something of a hustler. Like several other big-time cattlemen in the late 1870s, he paid cowhands to file for homesteads on land he wanted to acquire. He frequently hunted with Teddy Roosevelt, which certainly didn't hurt his chances of becoming superintendent of the Black Hills National Forest, not to mention his vacations to the White House. The fanciest old hotel in Deadwood still bears his name.

Bullock was always on the lookout for a deal. A 1908 book called *Wit and Humor in Business* tells the story of how Bullock, as a thirsty young placer gold miner in the 1860s, managed to "secure a fancy drink in the early days of Helena."

Entering the saloon one afternoon, Bullock told the bartender, "George, I'll tell you what let's do. If you will furnish the sherry, I'll furnish the fresh eggs, and we'll mix up a drink that is out of sight."

Liquor wasn't cheap, but eggs were even pricier — $2 a dozen — so the bartender thought that sounded like a bargain.

Bullock went to the grocer across the street and said to the proprietor, "Willard, if you'll furnish the eggs, I'll provide

Hot Springs promoters had the best marketing plan of any fledgling frontier town, claiming its mineral baths could cure a wide range of ailments.

the sherry, and we'll have something worthwhile in the line of fancy drinks." The grocer agreed, and the two went to the saloon, eggs in hand.

The concoction was duly prepared, and the three began to absorb it. Bullock had already swallowed his share when the bartender caught on. "Say," he demanded of Bullock, "Willard provided the eggs and I provided the liquor. Where do you come in on this deal?"

"Oh," Bullock replied. "I'm the promoter."

Promoters were a dime a dozen in Dakota's early days. Clawing out a living on the prairie was a bit easier if you had a mind for marketing and courage to go with it. Unfortunately, some savvy pioneers promoted products that didn't exist or towns that weren't quite as urbane as claimed. Others, like attorney Nelson J. Cramer, were opportunists who used laws

Katie Hunhoff

SEE FOR YOURSELF

Today, lovers of history can visit the Cramer-Kenyon house at 509 Pine Street in Yankton. The house is considered the tallest Queen Anne home in the state, and its style reflects efforts by a few wealthy newcomers to bring some East Coast sophistication to the rough and wild prairie.

to their advantage. Cramer bought more than a hundred farms and thousands of acres in southeast South Dakota although he never farmed an acre himself. During the farm depression of the 1890s he became famous (infamous in certain farm circles) for profiting from "snaps," a pioneer term for snapping up distressed farms. He acquired many of his holdings at foreclosure auctions.

Does that qualify Cramer as a rogue? It would if he snapped your family's farm. At the same time Cramer was snapping farms, across the state Fred Evans was scheming to ensure the railroad came to Hot Springs instead of Cascade, 10 miles south. The railroad eventually secured Hot Springs' future as well as Evans' fortune.

Evans came to the Hills in 1875 as a freighter but soon learned there were easier and more lucrative ways to make a living. He sold his freighting business and relocated to Hot Springs, guessing that the town could profit from the warm mineral baths nearby. The area was sought after years before Evans realized its value. The Lakota camped by the springs on the banks of the Fall River and they even battled the Cheyenne over the warm, clean waters.

Evans oversaw construction of many of Hot Springs' stately pink sandstone buildings — in fact, the sandstone came from his own quarry. Best known is the Evans Hotel which still stands in Hot Springs. He also was elected mayor, created the first electric plant, the first bank, planned the water system, organized a municipal band and built Evans Plunge.

It would be an understatement to say Evans was highly invested in Hot Springs. He realized, as the railroad was being built in 1890, that it must stop in Hot Springs or all his work would be for naught. Some people thought the picturesque town of Cascade, which also had warm mineral

Nelson J. Cramer was among the most disliked men in Yankton during the farm depression of the 1890s.

springs, would be a better railroad stop. Cascade was built with Chicago banking money, according to Hill City historian Watson Parker, "in the happy expectation that its warm springs and strategic location on the best possible railroad route into the

Fred Evans was a founding father of Hot Springs and went to great lengths to assure its survival.

Hills would transform it into a prosperous spa." Evans didn't like the sound of that.

In 1890, Danish immigrant and veteran stage driver Chris Jensen, who much later built the Blue Bell Lodge in what is now Custer State Park, decided to extend his stage line from Hot Springs to the resort at Cascade, where he hoped to lodge visitors.

Evans was also promoting Wind Cave, north of Hot Springs, as a tourist attraction. He decided to kill two birds with one stone. According to historian

MORE PRAIRIE PROMOTERS

EVERY PRAIRIE town promoter during the Great Dakota Boom of the 1880s swore their burg was going to be the next Chicago, so newspapermen A.B. Chubbuck and D.B. Worthington might have actually believed what they were saying. On August 16, 1884, they hailed the now-vanished Freeport (in Edmunds County) as the next Metropolis of the West and the "future grand railroad center of South Dakota." A month later they were asking all their friends to move with them to Ipswich, the NEXT great…

Evans Plunge was built in 1890 over several natural-fed springs. First hawked as a cure-all, the springs are now known for family fun.

John W. Bohl, Evans not only hired Jensen to haul visitors to Wind Cave. He also paid Jensen $250 a month not to take them to Cascade. But Evans wasn't the only man who liked to scheme; Jensen approached a rival stage line and sold his interest in the Cascade route for $300.

Cascade's death knell was the re-routing of the rail line. Meanwhile, Evans continued to build and promote Hot Springs. He died in 1902 in his favorite town.

Hucksterism was often practiced by snake oil salesmen, railroaders and local politicians with land to sell, but William Gage used the all-American art of salesmanship to attract bathers to the resorts at Hot Springs. As Evans secured the town's future, Gage tried to attract the world to the town with his outlandish claims.

Gage, a talented journalist, produced print ads and brochures for the Hot Springs Commercial Club, an early Chamber of Commerce that promoted the health benefits of the town's warm springs. One of his most imaginative stories told of 30 invalids from the Soldier's Home at Leavenworth, Kansas. All were Civil War veterans.

He wrote, "Feeble with the infirmities of age, and suffering from a variety of ailments, all but two were entirely cured and these two were greatly benefitted."

Gage said he personally observed cases, "where cripples were borne from the train in the arms of attendants and within a week were performing marvels of pedestrianism, alone and unattended."

The *Hot Springs Star* staff enjoyed the hot-water hoopla. In May of 1891 the editors reported on a particular cure: "A man, who was arraigned under the charge of being insane, waded in the river and got thoroughly wet, and when a board was appointed by Judge Cull to sit on the case, he suddenly recovered and attributes it all to the curative properties of Hot Springs waters."

Railroads could make or break fledgling prairie towns, so many conspiracies were designed to secure a railroad connection. Take the town of Minnesela for example. The town's promoters had the future all planned. Bring the Fremont, Elkhorn & Missouri Valley Railroad to town. Become a major cattle shipping point. Get rich.

Douglas Sayre heard of the plan and decided to get the jump on his fellow promoters. He skipped down to the Rapid City land office and filed a claim on the 80-acre parcel the railroad needed, then offered to sell it for $10,000.

Much to Minnesela's distress, the FE&MV passed and set up shop in Belle Fourche. Within a decade it was the world's busiest cattle shipping point and Minnesela had disappeared.

On the opposite side of the entrepreneurial spectrum was Odo Reder, a hardworking lumberjack. He wasn't a perpetual outlaw or huckster, only a lumberjack who didn't agree with a federal ban on cutting pines in the Black Hills.

"To cut or not to cut" the trees became an issue in the Hills very soon after white men arrived there. President Grover Cleveland created the Black Hills Forest Reserve in 1897 to conserve the pines.

South Dakota's politicians strenuously objected. U.S. Senator Freeman Knowles predicted that 15,000 people in the area

BEAUTY AND THE THIEVES

BELLE SIDDONS was born on a plantation in Missouri and raised as a southern belle. She possessed charm and social grace. It is rumored that during the Civil War, Siddons skillfully spied for the Confederacy, using her beauty and outgoing nature to learn secrets from Union officers.

After the war, Siddons learned to play cards and headed West where she opened her own gambling establishments. Calling herself Lurline Monte Verde, she eventually opened a gambling hall in Deadwood and dealt poker and faro. *Deadwood Magazine* wrote that Siddons was one of a kind. "She not only had resolve — she had the kind of flair and glamour that makes legends. Unfortunately, she also had a soft spot in her heart for those on the fringes of the law. It was a character flaw that would eventually lead to her downfall."

She fell into a relationship with Archie Cummings, the leader of a gang of thieves. Siddons used her charisma and looks to ferret out information useful to her beau's gang.

Several years later, the *Deadwood Daily Pioneer* reported the extent of her involvement in the gang by writing, "No robbery was undertaken of which she disapproved, and none failed in which she advised and planned the details."

Siddons' and Cummings' artful scheming couldn't go on forever. In 1877 bounty hunter Boone May learned of the pair's business relationship. He beat Siddons at her own game, sweet-talking her until he gathered enough evidence to arrest Cummings. He was hanged by vigilantes while being transported to Deadwood.

Siddons never recovered from the shock. She tried to poison herself, but survived. She then took up drinking and soon moved from the area. Some newspaper accounts noted her presence in Colorado, Arizona and finally in San Francisco, where they always mentioned her declining appearance. Who said beauty is a joy forever?

Photo courtesy of the Journey Museum

Odo Reder (second from left) wasn't a typical rogue, but he also didn't let a law get in the way of his timber sales.

would have to vacate their homes and become paupers.

The *Custer Chronicle* reported that, "consternation, wailing and gnashing of teeth was the order of the day ...." But Reder was undeterred by the president's order. He proceeded to illegally cut a half million feet of timber, according to the book *Sawmills of the Black Hills*.

Lumbermen came to Reder's defense, and one did so at the expense of other pioneers when he wrote, "The miner undermines the towns, pollutes streams and taints the very air of heaven with the smelter fumes; the stockman ranges his herds over Uncle Sam's fair green pastures until they are shorn and blackened wastes ... the sawmills make homes, schools and churches ... the sawmills are a potent civilizer."

Reder was fined $500. The ban was suspended in 1898.

South Dakota has an entrepreneurial history, and the tradition began with colorful and creative pioneers who were adept at pulling wool over their neighbors' eyes.

CHAPTER 14

Richard Pettigrew

Silver-Tongued Senator and Occasional Scoundrel

TWO DOCUMENTS HANG in the stairwell of Richard Pettigrew's meticulously-kept home at Eighth and Duluth in Sioux Falls. One is the Declaration of Independence, not surprising given Pettigrew was a career politician. The other is a federal indictment charging South Dakota's first full-term U.S. senator with violating the Espionage Act of 1917 for speaking against America's involvement in World War I.

Such a paper might shame many politicians, but the indictment became one of Pettigrew's most prized possessions, a symbol of his caustic tongue and brimming self confidence. His last will and testament, in which he bequeathed his home and all of its possessions to the city of Sioux Falls, stipulates that the indictment and the Declaration hang side by side forever.

Pettigrew played a major role in developing Sioux Falls and helping South Dakota gain admission to the Union as the 40th state. But his outspokenness, ever-changing opinions and willingness to adopt unpopular stances alienated him even among his allies. When he died in 1926, he had been all but forgotten for decades.

Richard Pettigrew was born July 23, 1848 in Ludlow, Vermont. His father was an ardent abolitionist who helped slaves escape from the South. Locals opposed to the elder Pettigrew's progressive attitude eventually drove the family from town.

Part of Richard Pettigrew's home at Eighth and Duluth in Sioux Falls was built with petrified logs from Arizona before it became illegal to scavenge the wood.

They moved to Wisconsin in 1854, where Pettigrew's father worked a small farm. Richard enrolled at Beloit College, but after his father's death he returned to help run the family farm. As he toiled he dreamt of a professional career, and passed exams to become a teacher. He studied law books while teaching, and in 1868 entered law school at the University of Wisconsin in Madison. But a year later, eager to find his fortune in the West, he joined a surveying crew and departed for Dakota Territory.

Sioux Falls was beginning its second life when Pettigrew arrived. Founded a decade earlier, settlers abandoned the town site during the Sioux Wars of the early 1860s. They returned after the U.S. military established Fort Dakota to protect pioneers from Indian attacks. Pettigrew claimed 160 acres and returned permanently the following year, intent on making the village succeed.

His ambition trumped compliance with the law when the federal government announced plans in 1870 to close Fort Dakota. Pettigrew, already with an eye on politics, told people living within Fort Dakota that they would have first claim to land within its boundaries as soon as the land was surveyed.

Senator Pettigrew drew charges of fraud in both his business and political careers.

But then he learned that a group of investors led by Wilmot W. Brookings planned to buy all the military land in Minnehaha County. Pettigrew and Nyrum Phillips, wanting to control settlement in the old military fort, drafted a petition seeking to delay the sale of Fort Dakota's land. They soon discovered that too few people lived within Minnehaha County to sign it, so Pettigrew and Phillips added names of men they thought would soon settle in the county, and sent it to Pettigrew's friend, Sen. Matthew Carpenter of

Wisconsin. Carpenter convinced Congress to comply, delaying the opening and allowing Pettigrew and Phillips to dictate who settled at old Fort Dakota.

Pettigrew knew how to maximize his connections. He purchased a parcel of land, but through the vagaries of 19th century documentation and a muddled passing of titles, a Minneapolis man claimed to own the same property. A trip to Minnesota was required to set the matter straight. Pettigrew secured a deed, but on the way home he spotted an attorney representing his opponent aboard the train. He surmised that the man had likely gotten another deed, so it became a race to the Minnehaha County courthouse. Pettigrew knew the engineer and conductor, and he convinced them to stop the train four miles from Sioux Falls and claim to have run out of water. Pettigrew then rode the engine into town and filed his deed. The attorney arrived 30 minutes later, only to find the land had already been awarded to Pettigrew.

Despite his chicanery, Pettigrew was committed to growing Sioux Falls. He helped bring five railroad lines into the young city, and formed his own railroad and trolley companies with his brother, Fred. His biggest dream was creating a transcontinental railroad running from Sioux Falls to Seattle. Among his more controversial investments was the state of the art, seven-story Queen Bee Mill, whose remains still stand along the banks of the Big Sioux River in Falls Park.

Stories circulated for years claiming that Pettigrew dammed the Big Sioux River in order to build the mill. Shortly after construction finished in 1881, Pettigrew and his partners realized there wouldn't be enough waterpower or wheat to keep it running. He convinced wealthy New York financier George Seney to invest in the project. Legend says that to impress Seney, Pettigrew dammed the river, then released a rush of water as Seney toured the site. Historians have since disproven the popular myth.

As he helped build Sioux Falls, Pettigrew developed an itch for politics. He lost his first bid for a seat in the territorial

House of Representatives in 1870. He ran again in 1872 and won, but suspicion clouded his campaign and he was eventually thrown out of the legislature. Pettigrew's district encompassed Minnehaha, Lincoln, Turner, Brookings and Deuel counties, a vast tract of land surrounding Sioux Falls. Few settlers lived in the far northern reaches of the district where the town of Gary, straddling the Minnesota border, was just developing. Many of its residents were nomadic workers laying railroad track. Pettigrew had met them while surveying there in the summer.

In September a friend of Pettigrew's passed through Sioux Falls on his way to Deuel County to establish voting districts. Pettigrew noticed that the ballots he carried for the upcoming election did not include his name. The candidate hastily printed a new batch with his name included, and apparently in some portions of the county these were the only ballots used. He received 592 votes, second most in his district and enough to win a spot in the legislature.

Pettigrew took his seat at the capital in Yankton, but the results were challenged just three days after the election. A divided House committee issued two reports: one recommended Pettigrew stay, the other favored his removal. The full House voted to oust Pettigrew, and the "Deuel County Fraud" incident haunted him for the rest of his life.

Pettigrew finally won a seat in the legislature in 1874. During his time as a territorial lawmaker, he helped make Sioux Falls the seat of Minnehaha County and wrote a bill creating Lake and Moody counties. To his benefit, Pettigrew ensured that Flandreau became the Moody County seat. He and his brother, Fred, owned large tracts of land there.

In 1880 Pettigrew ran for Congress. His quick thinking and silver tongue helped him escape an alarming situation while campaigning in the Black Hills. The stagecoach trail to Deadwood was notoriously dangerous. Outlaws frequently robbed the coach near Buffalo Gap. Pettigrew sought to avoid violence. He pleaded with fellow travelers not to fight if they were robbed, and convinced them to stash their firearms in their travel bags.

As the stagecoach neared Buffalo Gap, a band of robbers, as if on cue, rushed the coach. Passengers were ordered outside and forced to surrender their money and valuables. Pettigrew carefully studied one of the masked men who robbed him of $17, plus a silver watch and chain. To the robber's surprise, Pettigrew whispered, "Kemsley, what shall I tell your mother?"

Pettigrew recognized Kemsley Towles, whose family farmed about six miles outside of Sioux Falls. Kemsley, an awkward 18-year-old, had left the farm for the Hills, eager to strike it rich during the gold rush. But fortune eluded him and he turned to crime.

"You didn't see me," replied the startled Towles, and discreetly returned Pettigrew's money and watch. He joined his partners and sped away on horseback.

The stunned passengers glanced at one another in disbelief. Then their suspicious eyes turned to Pettigrew. Earlier in the journey he had persuaded them to put away their weapons. Now, he was the only one among them who hadn't been robbed. Was he part of the heist?

Pettigrew deftly dissolved the tension. He glibly explained why his possessions were returned, then convinced them they had just been robbed by the notoriously violent Lame Johnny Gang. Luckily their weapons were safely out of reach, he said, because if anyone had drawn a gun in self-defense they all would have been killed.

Pettigrew won the election and served one term as Dakota Territory's delegate in Congress, where he secured funds to build the state penitentiary in Sioux Falls. He also strongly supported division of Dakota Territory and statehood for the southern half, a cause that endeared him to people living south of the 46th parallel (today's North Dakota/South Dakota border). When South Dakota gained statehood in 1889, the legislature elected the Republican Pettigrew the state's first full-term U.S. Senator.

In Washington, Pettigrew secured funding for some of Sioux Falls' landmark buildings, including the federal courthouse and post office building (which he insisted be built from native Sioux quartzite) at 12th Street and Phillips Avenue. Unfortunately the economically turbulent 1890s affected Pettigrew's political and professional life. His trolley company went bankrupt and the rail line to the West Coast fell through. It marked the beginning of a drastic change in Pettigrew. He began to question capitalism and lost trust in the country's business leaders, many of whom comprised the core of the Republican Party. Pettigrew saw a solution to the country's economic woes in the free and unlimited coinage of silver, and in 1896 he bolted the Republican Party to become a Silver Republican and, eventually, a Populist.

The move put him at odds with President William McKinley, and their relationship worsened over the next four years. Pettigrew was a vocal opponent of the Spanish-American War, despite strong support across the country. He was also an outspoken anti-imperialist, opposing the United States' annexation of the Philippines and the Hawaiian Islands. Pettigrew openly criticized the president and military leaders, and called the American flag a "rag" — comments that were not well received by South Dakotans. Pettigrew became such a thorn in McKinley's side that Ohio Sen. Mark Hanna, McKinley's presidential campaign manager in 1900, said he had two goals that year: to re-elect McKinley and defeat Pettigrew, "and I did not know which I wanted worst." He got both. Thanks to a well-organized fund-raising drive within the national Republican Party that pumped nearly $500,000 into South Dakota, Pettigrew lost his bid for re-election.

Pettigrew joined the Democratic Party and split time between Sioux Falls and New York City. In 1912, he supported the Progressives and their presidential candidate Theodore Roosevelt. After Roosevelt's defeat, Pettigrew's politics became even more radical. He flirted with Socialism and Communism and wrote two books that drew praise from Soviet leaders Vladimir Lenin and Leon Trotsky.

He endured much criticism in 1917 for uttering statements against the United States' involvement in World War I. He told an *Argus Leader* reporter that the war was simply a capitalist scheme to make the rich even richer, and he urged young men to avoid the draft. *Argus* editors passed the comments to the U.S. Attorney, who charged Pettigrew with violating the Espionage Act, a measure that outlawed even the faintest criticism about World War I.

Pettigrew faced a stiff penalty. Socialist leader Eugene Debs, also indicted under the Espionage Act, served three years of a 10-year prison sentence. Pettigrew assembled a legal team headlined by his close friend Clarence Darrow. Delays kept the case out of court, and eventually the charges were dropped.

By then, Pettigrew had fallen out of favor with nearly everyone in Sioux Falls. He died at his home on Oct. 5, 1926, and was entombed at Woodlawn Cemetery.

Negative stories about Pettigrew circulated long after his death. His home — the only physical reminder of his life and work — was nothing more than a hodgepodge of artifacts with no interpretation. But Pettigrew has enjoyed a resurgence in recent years. Siouxland Heritage Museums turned his home into a popular attraction. His old neighborhood was christened Pettigrew Heights, and an elementary school named for him opened in 2009. Volunteers led a fundraising effort to refurbish his mausoleum, and a sculpture of Pettigrew is planned for downtown overlooking Falls Park. Pettigrew's contemporaries may have kept their distance from the prickly politician, but their descendants are embracing his role in shaping South Dakota and helping Sioux Falls become its urban center.

Richard Pettigrew

PETTIGREW'S LOG HOUSE

PART OF RICHARD PETTIGREW'S Queen Anne style home at the corner of Eighth Street and Duluth Avenue in Sioux Falls was built using 200-million-year-old logs from Arizona, gleaned before it became a federal crime to harvest the ancient treasures.

In the early 1900s, Pettigrew heard about the amazing bounty of petrified wood in Arizona. He had tons of rocks shipped to Sioux Falls. When President Theodore Roosevelt heard of the damage that artifact hunters like Pettigrew were doing, he convinced Congress to create the Arizona Petrified Forest National Park in 1906.

Pettigrew hoped to sell the petrified logs, but a plan never materialized. Instead, they were used in construction. Some logs became part of a huge arch at Woodlawn Cemetery. Other pieces were used to build an addition to his home in 1923, which houses a vast collection of artifacts.

Pettigrew and his brother Fred were avid amateur archae-ologists. They regularly visited the site of the ancient Blood Run Indian village along the South Dakota/Iowa border north of Canton to search for artifacts. Pettigrew also collected thousands of items from around the world during his two terms as a U.S. Senator. Items on display include a piece of the Great Pyramid, a bottle of water from the Jordan River and a collection of canes, one of which was a gift from Hawaiian Queen Liliuokalani.

The Pettigrew Home and Museum is open daily. Call (605) 367-7097 for hours or to arrange a tour.

CHAPTER 15

The Death of LeBeau

Did a Cattle Baron Burn the Town?

WHAT KILLED LEBEAU?

Did a bridge at Mobridge or the shooting of a rich rancher's son kill the little town on the east bank of the Missouri?

It can be hard to separate the rogue, the hero and the victim in some Old West stories. That's especially true when cattle, cowboys, guns and whiskey are involved.

Such an incident unraveled in LeBeau on the morning of Dec. 11, 1909 when Dode MacKenzie, the fun-loving and hard-drinking son of Scottish cattle baron Murdo MacKenzie, was shot three times in the chest. The assailant was Bud Stephens, an aging cowboy who bartended in the Angel Bar, which was operated by Phil DuFran.

The town of LeBeau took root in 1875 as a fur-trading post on the Missouri, some 70 miles north of Pierre. The town was formed in 1883, but it grew slowly until 1904 when several million acres on the Cheyenne and Standing Rock Indian reservations were opened to grazing for just 3.5 cents per acre. The West's big cattle barons arrived to compete for the rich native grasses, often to the chagrin of homesteaders and other dirt farmers.

Grass-fat steers were worth $45 in Chicago in 1907, so the South Dakota beef industry soon attracted the attention of the Milwaukee and St. Louis Railroad and in 1906 a track reached the east bank of the Missouri River at Swan Creek. It missed LeBeau by two miles, but the town leaders were flexible. They

packed up and moved to the railhead.

West River cattle from the reservations and from southern states were ferried across the river when it was too high to ford. More than 150,000 head were herded onto train cars in LeBeau for delivery to Minneapolis, Chicago and other eastern cities in the fall of 1909.

As winter arrived on the prairie, LeBeau was abuzz with bawling cattle and noisy, fun-loving cowboys. It now had two churches, a bakery, drug store, newspaper and numerous saloons. Hotel LeBeau bragged of steam heat, and dogs were not allowed in the sleeping rooms. Several churches were built, and Zimmer's Opera House offered theater and music.

The Angel Bar was the unofficial headquarters of the Mata-

LeBeau, on the eastern bank of the Missouri River, was poised to become a major cattle shipping point until two mysterious fires destroyed the town.

dor Land and Cattle Company, run by Murdo MacKenzie. He was born in Scotland, but sailed to America in 1885 and made a fortune in cattle. He was a friend of President Teddy Roosevelt and founder of the American Stock Growers Association.

Conflicting stories were told about the lead-up to the Dec. 11 shooting. Some cowboys teased Dode MacKenzie that Stephens, a former Matador cowpoke, was out to get him. An argument had apparently occurred earlier between the young MacKenzie and Stephens, who was described as "a short, mustached, bow-legged, half-deaf old cowhand."

MacKenzie and Stephens exchanged angry words in the bar

Cattlemen conducted business by day in LeBeau, but they could grow rowdy at the Angel Bar, where Bud Stephens killed Dode MacKenzie.

on that fateful day, and then — by one account — MacKenzie walked across the street to Knoll's Hardware and bought a Colt .45 revolver. As the story goes, he bought a handful of .38 caliber cartridges that, of course, would be useless in the Colt.

Dode supposedly took the unloaded gun from his overcoat pocket and placed it on the bar. A friend told him it was foolish to threaten Stephens with a pistol that couldn't fire.

"Don't worry about this old drunk," said Dode's friend. "We'll take care of him later."

Dode agreed. "We'll have no trouble in your place," he told Stephens. "But be ready if you leave."

Phil DuFran, a survivor of the infamous Johnson County Range War in Wyoming 18 years earlier, wanted no trouble with big ranchers like the MacKenzies. He ordered Stephens to the back room. Stephens started to retreat, then reached beneath the counter, pulled out a .44 caliber and fired three shots pointblank into Dode MacKenzie's chest.

The heir to the Matador kingdom collapsed and was soon declared dead. He was just 31.

Stephens surrendered to the town constable and was whisked away to the new courthouse at Selby to avoid a lynch mob. The barkeep was assigned two court appointed attorneys, E.P. Harkin of Aberdeen and Pat Morrison of Mobridge.

They faced off against a battery of high-powered lawyers hired to assist the Walworth County states attorney by a grief-stricken Murdo MacKenzie, who wanted justice for his son. The cattle baron didn't attend the trial. He probably felt it was a cut-and-dry case of first degree murder.

Morrison, just 23 years old, was already savvy enough to recognize the Walworth County homesteaders' dislike for the big cattle barons, so he stacked the jury box with farmers.

Morrison's son, Pat Jr., heard stories about the case while growing up in Mobridge. He told *South Dakota Magazine* in 2012 that his dad graduated from law school at the University of Minnesota and got on a train headed west. "Every time the train stopped, he got off and asked if the town had a lawyer. When the train stopped at Mobridge, he got off and asked and they told him they needed him." The MacKenzie shooting happened about a year later.

Jurors weighed Stephens' claim of self-defense against the prosecutors' story of a cold-blooded murder. Maybe it was the defense's passionate two-hour closing argument, or tension between cattle kings and small farmers. Or maybe they simply felt Stephens had a right to feel threatened. For whatever reason, the verdict was innocent. Morrison gained an instant reputation, and soon became known as one of South Dakota's best criminal lawyers.

Some believe Murdo MacKenzie, head of the Matador Land and Cattle Company, ordered LeBeau burned after his son's murder.

"The jury bought self defense," said his son. "The old man got back to Mobridge and they had a big banquet for him, honoring him for winning the trial like a town might honor a team for winning the State B tournament."

In a distinguished career that continued into the 1960s, Morrison defended 10 men and women in first degree murder trials. All 10 were acquitted, said his son, a renowned radio broadcaster. "The old man in his lifetime was a real legend. He was a colorful person in the courtroom, though I suppose they wouldn't allow some of his antics today."

The story of LeBeau and the MacKenzies has been told and retold in many Old West history books. There are few discrepancies. One thing is certain: Murdo MacKenzie and the Matador cowboys pulled all support from the town. The ranch headquarters was moved to Whitehorse and Mobridge became the new railhead when the Milwaukee and St. Paul built a rail bridge across the Missouri. Not a single Matador steer or cowboy ever again stepped foot in LeBeau.

It's also a matter of fact that LeBeau's business district suffered a devastating fire in September of 1910, just six months after the jury verdict — and then another fire after that.

The first blaze — which quickly turned most of Main Street to ashes — seemed suspicious. Some historical writers claim that the volunteer fire department rushed to extinguish the flames, only to find their hoses had been cut into pieces. Then they tried to wire for help, but the telegraph lines had been cut.

"The street where MacKenzie had died was brightly illuminated by the flaming buildings which flanked it," wrote Bob Lee in his classic history, *Last Grass Frontier.* "Ironically, Du-Fran's saloon was one of the three buildings on the street that survived."

"Nobody had any proof," said Pat Morrison Jr., but the common belief was that Murdo MacKenzie or his cowboys retaliated against the town for the death of Dode MacKenzie.

Ike Blasingame, a Matador ranch hand, wrote of his experiences on the South Dakota range many years later. His book, *Dakota Cowboy,* is considered both entertaining and accurate. Though Blasingame was an admirer of the MacKenzies, some historians believe that he would have divulged any knowledge of arson.

A paragraph in the book could be so construed. "The pale hand of retribution even then began spreading the shroud, as ghostly wings hovered over the lusty, hard-bitten town, deeming its doom," wrote Blasingame. "A few months after Dode died in her streets, the first lethal blow fell upon LeBeau. Fire started on Main Street and raced through most of her business section — a loss estimated at two hundred thousand dollars."

Beyond that, Blasingame gave no indication that arson was the cause of the fire, or that his old boss was to blame. Subtlety was hardly the old cowboy's writing style. Historians love *Dakota Cowboy* because of Blasingame's no-nonsense approach.

Blasingame did have an opinion on Stephens' guilt. "It seemed incredible that anyone would want to kill Dode," he wrote. "Walter McDonald, who stood next to Dode and saw Bud Stephens shoot him full of lead, told me about it. He said that Dode had not even hinted harm to Bud.

"Whatever he may have said to the man was of a rough, rollicky nature such as was Dode's custom with all, for he was a friendly man. His one weakness was drink, but even then he wasn't mean."

After the shooting, wrote Blasingame, "No Matador cowboy ever again trod in her streets in the same friendliness as before. All of us knew the deep personal grief our chief, Murdo MacKenzie, had suffered over his beloved David — Dode — good cowboy and always one of us, regardless of his position as Murdo's son.

"What was left of LeBeau after the first fire was wiped out by a second fire a few months later," he continued, "and after that she ceased to exist — only in caved-in cellars, crumbling sidewalks and broken brick, all of it weed-grown and lonely. Even the railroad tracks were pulled up. Nothing remains."

Bud Stephens hung around Mobridge for a time, and then left the area. "The story goes that he drifted away, and then they found him out in Montana in a field, dead," Morrison said, recalling stories from his father. "They felt Murdo MacKenzie had the last word on that, but again that was never confirmed."

LeBeau got a proper burial 50 years later when the Oahe Dam was completed in 1962 and the huge reservoir known as Lake Oahe began to fill, flooding the town site. The town now lies, nearly forgotten, under the world's fourth-largest manmade lake. Bud Stephens' .44 can be seen in the Walworth County Courthouse at nearby Selby. Some summers, when the lake level is low, a few concrete steps and foundation stones appear on the water's edge.

CHAPTER 16

Calamity Jane
The Legend and the Lout

MARTHA JANE Cannary was notorious for confusing fact with fiction when it came to tales told of her life, but she might have saved herself the trouble: the true, unvarnished story is entertaining enough.

Jane was born in Missouri in 1856, and moved to Montana Territory with her parents and five younger siblings toward the end of the Civil War. Charlotte Cannary died before they reached Billings, and Robert Cannary never found gold there, or anywhere else he looked; when he died all he left 15-year-old Jane were his nomadic inclinations and the need to fend for herself. "[She] soon acquired bad habits like drinking, smoking, cursing and wearing pants," wrote one wag. Several stretches in jail failed to change her ways, and before long young Martha completed her turn off the straight and narrow by becoming a prostitute.

Jane spent the next few years drifting across the West, from mining camps to military posts to ever-moving railroad towns, plying her chosen trade between stints of more reputable labor as a cook and seamstress. She was living near Fort Laramie, Wyoming, in 1875 when the expedition led by Henry Newton and Walter Jenney left for its historic geological survey of the Black Hills. Jane, who was nothing if not adventurous, invited herself along.

She served as a scout for the party's Army escort, according

Cannary was treated like a star when she returned to Deadwood in 1895 after a long absence. She lived off her notoriety until her death eight years later.

to an autobiography, but that was a complete fabrication. In his dispatches on the Newton-Jenney expedition, a reporter for the *Chicago Inter-Ocean* wrote of "a strange creature" named Calamity who dressed like a soldier, rode straight up instead of side-saddle like the women back East, and was an expert mule-skinner. (There are at least three stories of how Martha became Calamity Jane. In the sympathetic version, she acquired the name by virtue of the calamity of being orphaned at a young age; at the other end of the spectrum, it was suggested that the men who sampled her charms afterward suffered the calamity of a social disease. Jane herself invented a tale in which she earned the title by saving an Army officer, Captain James Egan, from certain calamity at the hands of Indians. No one really knows.)

Dr. Valentine McGillycuddy's recollection of Jane agreed with the newspaper report generally, though not in every particular. She disguised herself as an Army private in order to join the expedition, according to McGillycuddy, and when she was unmasked as a camp follower — a woman who sewed and cooked and provided intimate services for soldiers — Col. Richard Dodge banished her from his command. That proved to be only a temporary inconvenience for Jane, who circumvented his order by signing on with the party's teamsters and finishing the trip.

Calamity Jane returned to the Hills the following summer, on the same wagon train as Charles "Colorado Charlie" Utter, James "Wild Bill" Hickok, "and a few other dissolute characters who had been asked to leave Cheyenne," wrote Watson Parker in *Deadwood, The Golden Years*. Scriptwriters for the HBO series *Deadwood* are the latest in a long line who have been unable to resist the urge to link Calamity Jane and Wild Bill, but they were actually no more than passing acquaintances; a friend of Utter's even claimed that Jane's true romantic interest was none other than Colorado Charlie.

Dora DuFran, the longtime Black Hills madam, didn't meet Calamity Jane until the mid-1880s, but her description of Jane probably applied at the height of the Gold Rush. "Her face was deeply pitted from smallpox, tanned until it looked like leather," wrote Dora in *Low Down on Calamity Jane*. "Her hair was black and straight as an Indian's. She wore it parted in the middle and coiled low on the neck." Another observer called her, "about the roughest looking human being I ever saw," which was saying something considering the rugged characters who called Deadwood home.

There were roughly 5,000 men in Deadwood that summer. Jane was one of the few women around and would have been quite popular regardless of her grooming, but she still felt obliged to make an effort. Joseph "White Eye" Anderson later told the story of loaning Jane $20 so she could buy a dress. Once suitably attired, Calamity joined seven other working girls in a hotel owned by a gambler named Porter.

During her first stretch in Deadwood, from 1876 to 1881, Jane worked in various dance halls and sporting houses, waiting tables or whoring as the night required. She operated her own restaurant for a time, then tried her hand at running a brothel and a saloon, which failed, "because she was her own best customer," as DuFran put it. Calamity also labored as a bull-whacker on the Fort Pierre to Deadwood Trail, making her one of the only women who could cite both teamster and prostitute on their resume.

Every town in the West had its own painted-lady-with-a-heart-of-gold story, and in Deadwood the lady was Calamity Jane. DuFran characterized Jane as "an ignorant, uneducated, untamed, immoral, iron-hearted woman," and in the very next breath "a ministering angel" of the frontier, ever ready, "to do some poor soul a favor, to buy a meal for a down-and-outer, to pay the wash bill of some unlucky sister."

Deadwood historians would grant DuFran both halves of that description, even if they weren't quite as willing to accord Calamity sainthood. "Admirers have claimed that Calamity Jane nursed some of the smallpox victims [during the epidemic of 1878], and she probably did, being a woman of generous inclinations and noted for her disregard of any and all the dangers of her profession," wrote Watson Parker, "but her detractors murmured that if indeed she cured any smallpox victims she probably gave them the great pox in return."

Her good deeds also provided good excuses. Accused of robbing a male customer, Calamity admitted as much, and then explained to the judge that she had only done it to pay for treating a sick girl.

Honorable deeds alone don't account for her place among Deadwood's most memorable characters. She is remembered for being wild-eyed, rip-roaring and foul-mouthed — a don't-give-a-damn outlook on convention which came to the fore and was magnified whenever she was drunk, which she quite often was. Calamity Jane was almost certainly an alcoholic from her teenage years on, and by the time she reached adulthood her capacity for liquor was legendary.

Calamity Jane was photographed in Pierre in 1901 after returning from the East Coast.

"'Give me a shot of booze and slop her over the brim' was her standing order when invited for a drink," according to Dora Du-Fran.

Newspaperman Leander P. Richardson visited Deadwood in the summer of 1876, and later recalled an evening when Calamity consumed enough whiskey "to awaken her ambition," then mounted a horse "man fashion" and tore up and down the street, howling like an inebriated coyote. "As a fitting wind-up for that harmless little burst of innocent enthusiasm … she shot out the windows of a dance hall owned by Miss Kitty Arnold."

When on a binge, Calamity would pass out somewhere convenient, wake up the next morning and start all over, sometimes for days on end. She was in the midst of such a tear the first time she met DuFran. "Jane had been drunk for more than a week and had become rather tired," DuFran recalled. "She was sitting down on the curb with her feet in a stream of water which ran down both sides of Main Street. Her head was held up by her hands, elbows on knees. Jane was taking a nap."

Calamity Jane the character was more celebrated the further away one got from firsthand knowledge. Barely a year after she arrived in Deadwood, a local newspaper editor denounced her as a fraud, no doubt for her tendency to fabricate tall tales. Yet for the remainder of her days, those stories were Calamity Jane's stock-in-trade. She left Deadwood in 1881 and resumed her tumbleweed ways, visiting old haunts and new boomtowns, telling and retelling and embellishing as she went.

Jane's reputation as a western character was given a huge

SEE FOR YOURSELF

Were Calamity Jane and Wild Bill Hickok lovers? Books, movies and television shows have long sought to link the two, but historians have discovered they were no more than passing acquaintances. Still, Calamity did nothing to dispel the myth. She posed for photographs by Wild Bill's grave following his death in 1876 and boasted to reporters (wrongly) that she played a key role in apprehending Jack McCall (Wild Bill's killer), and in his trial and hanging in Yankton.

Before she died in 1903, Calamity Jane requested to be buried next to Wild Bill Hickok in Deadwood's Mount Moriah Cemetery. Deadwood promoters liked the idea because they thought the story would be good for business. They remain side by side to this day. Admission to Mount Moriah is $1. Call (605) 722-0837 for information.

boost when Edward Wheeler issued the first installment of *Deadwood Dick's Doom, or Calamity Jane's Last Adventure* in 1877. Wheeler apparently never consulted Jane before writing her into his narrative as, "the notorious free-and-easy reckless waif of the rocky Western country" and Deadwood Dick's "truest pard for many a year," but there is no such thing as bad publicity. Wheeler's inventions were added to her own considerable lies, and by 1896 Calamity was a household name and featured performer at the Palace Museum in Minneapolis. A ghostwriter with the firm penned her "autobiography" publicity for the show, and Jane's imaginary exploits spread.

At some point after she left Deadwood, Jane met a man named Burke. She took his name — Martha Jane Burke is the name on her tombstone in Deadwood's Mount Moriah Cemetery — even though they may not have been formally married. She had at least one child with him or another of the many other men she lived with over the years, but motherhood didn't slow her down. In 1902, when she was showing the wear of her 56 years, Jane was thrown into the Billings jail for getting drunk and threatening a woman with a hatchet.

Calamity Jane let it be known that she would never return to Billings after that miscarriage of justice. She returned to Deadwood, and shortly after the turn of 1903, she settled in Belle Fourche, "apparently determined to turn over a new leaf," according to her biographer James McLaird. Dora DuFran took her on as cook at her brothel. Things went well for about six weeks, which was as long as Jane ever stayed sober, according to DuFran, then she was off on a five-day binge.

By mid-March Jane was on the move again. In retrospect, her last months were like a victory lap. She floated from Deadwood to Lead to Spearfish to Sundance, Wyoming, and no matter where she stopped there was always someone willing to put her up, pay for drinks, listen and gawk at the notorious Calamity Jane. "There is hardly enough rubber … in people's necks to allow them to stretch far enough to get a good look at Jane," reported the *Daily Journal* on her visit to Rapid City.

Martha Jane Cannary Burke made her final visit to Deadwood in late July. There were too many ghosts about, or perhaps the old gold rush town had become too civilized for her taste. She soon departed by train for Terry, and not long after the *Lead Daily Call* reported that "the heroine of many a lurid tale of the Black Hills" was gravely ill.

Calamity Jane passed away on August 1, 1903, but her long, tall tales of the Old West and the Days of '76 may live forever.

Adams Museum 37, 86
Allen, A.J. 59-66
American Fur Company 11
Ardmore 70
Arnold, Kitty 54
Ash, Henry 44
Astor, John Jacob 12
Barnes, A.H. 5
Barnett, Gene 73-74, 79
Bass, Sam 32-34
Beadle, William Henry
Harrison 42-43
Belle Fourche 29-31, 51-52, 137
Bennett, Granville 42
Berry, Jim 32
Big Hat Clark 82, 84
Big Sioux River 116
Bismarck Anne 52
Black Elk 81
Blackbird, Joe 99
Blasingame, Ike 128-130
Blood Run 121
Bonesteel 14, 98
Born, Dutch Henry 36-37
Boyles, Virgil & Kate 101
Bradley, Henry 13
Briggs, Marie 49-50
Brookings, Wilmot W. 115
Brown, H.E. 35
Brown, Jesse 74, 76
Buffalo Gap 76, 79, 117-118
Bullock, Seth 25, 37, 78,
105-106
Bulow, William 93
Burbank, John A. 4-6
Burdick, J.H. 39, 42-43
Burleigh, Robert 62-63
Burleigh, Walter 2-4, 6
Campbell, Charles 14
Campbell, Hugh 74
Calamity Jane 54, 91, 131-138
Canton 121
Carey, Charles 78-79
Carpenter, Matthew 115-116

Cascade 107-109
Casey, Robert 60
Castle Creek 75
Charles Mix County 11, 96
Chouteau, Pierre 12
Chubbuck, A.B. 108
Cleveland, Grover 110
Cody, William 69
Collins, Joel 32-33
Cook, Ed 61, 76
Cramer, Nelson J. 106-107
Crawford, Jack 46-47
Cricket Saloon 21
Crook, George 20
Cummings, Archie 111
Curry, Henry 63
Curry, Louis 59-66
Custer 20-21, 53, 78
Custer County 6, 75
Custer Expedition 81
Custer, George 14, 30, 36
Custer State Park 108
Dakota Southern Railway Co. 5
Darrow, Clarence 120
Davie, William 20
Davis, Jack 33
Davis, Scott 74
Daxacher, John 39, 43
Deadwood 17-27, 30-37,
39-45, 49-58, 73-79, 101,
111, 117, 133-138
Debs, Eugene 120
Deuel County 117
Diamond, Ben 100
Dodge, Richard 133
DuCharme, Cuthbert 11-16, 96
Duffield, Frank 90
DuFran, Dora 50-52, 133-137
DuFran, Phil 123
Dumont, Eleanor 55
Edmunds County 108
Edmunds, Newton 4
Egan, James 133
Ellis, Joe 99

Evans, Fred 107-109
Everett, Jack 93
Faulk, Andrew 3-4, 6
Faulk, Phil 43-44
Fielder, Mildred 59-66
Finstad, Olaf 99, 103
Flormann, Robert 85
Fort Dakota 115
Fort Meade 53, 91
Fort Pierre 12
Fort Randall 1, 12
Freeport 108
Gage, William 109-110
Gary 117
Geddes 11, 15-16
Giles, Al 29, 31
Grant, Ulysses S. 43, 96
Gregory County 95-103
Hall, James 60-66
Halstead, Orval 79
Ham, Harry 99, 101
Hanna, Mark 119
Harkin, E.P. 126
Harney Peak 81
Harney Stage 81-82
Harris, Frank 76
Hawthorne, Mont 60
Hayward 81
Henry, George 86-87
Henry, Robert 87
Hickok, Wild Bill 21, 39-45,
54-55, 133, 136
Hill City 53
Hill, Fanny 56, 58
Hill, Galen 73
Holliday, Pam 57
Homestake Gold Mine 73, 78
Hot Springs 107-110
Howard, William A. 6-7, 78
Huckert, George 93
Ipswich 108
Irwin, John 34
Jayne, William 2
Jennack, John 62

Index

Jenney, Walter 81, 131
Jensen, Chris 108-109
Johnson, Mollie 55-56
Keystone 52-53, 82
Kickland, Ryan 103
Kincaid, Mary Goulette 97, 100
Knowles, Freeman 110
Laflin, Matthew 85-86
Lake Andes 99
Lame Johnny 74-79
Latimer, George 21
Lawrence County 6
Lead 51, 73
LeBeau 123-130
Lillibridge, William 101
Link, Lawrence 45
Lucas 97
Luse, Julius 12
Mackenzie, Alexander 10
MacKenzie, Dode 123-129
MacKenzie, Murdo 123-129
Mann, Carl 40, 43
Mansfield, Bill 78
Marble, Art 29, 31
Marble, David 61
Marr, Johnny 21
Massie, William 40-41, 43
May, Boone 34-36, 74, 76-78
McBride, Frank 78
McCall, Jack 21, 39-45, 136
McClintock, John S. 59
McCook, Edwin 5
McDaniels, James 41
McGillycuddy, Valentine 133
McKimie, Reddy 32
McKinley, William 119
McLaughlin, Archie 78
McMullen, James 98
Metz, Charles 35
Mickelson, George 94
Middleton, Doc 67-71
Miner, William 73-74
Minnehaha County 115-117
Minnesela 110

Missouri Fur Company 11
Missouri River 11
Montague, Harry 22-23
Moore, Tom 76
Moses, George 91
Moulton, Frank 61-63
Murphy, John Francis 75
Nelson, James 85
Newton, Henry 131
Niobrara River 69
Nixon, Tom 32
Oahe Dam 130
O'Day, Tom 30-31
Oelrichs 70
Old Man Wright 65-66
Ordway, Nehemiah G. 7-10
Oslund, Pete 77
Pam's Purple Door 57
Papineau Flats 14
Parks, Annie 53
Pastor, Tony 75-76
Pennington County 6
Pennington, John L. 6
Persimmon Bill 34-36
Petrie, John 95, 99-101
Pettigrew Heights 120
Pettigrew, Richard 7, 113-121
Phillips, Nyrum 115-116
Pinney, George M. 2
Poker Alice 53, 89-94
Potato Creek Johnny 86
Quinn, Jim 94
Rapid City 6, 50-52, 59-66, 82
Red Canyon 35
Red Cloud Agency 75
Red Rock 98
Reder, Odo 110-112
Rich, Charles 40
Richardson, Leander 54-55, 135
Richardson, Rene 70-71
Saloon No. 10 40-41
Sample, Bill 74
Sayre, Douglas 110
Seim, Olaf 85

Selby 130
Seney, George 116
Shannon, Oliver 42-43
Shannon, P.C. 43
Shingle, George 41, 43
Siddons, Belle 111
Sioux Falls 113-121
Slaughter, Johnny 32-33
Smith, Billy 63-64
Smith, Ellison 13
Smith, Eugene 74
Smith, James 76
Sommereisen, Valentine 45
Starcher 98
Stephens, Bud 123-130
Sturgis 53, 89-94
Sully, Alfred 14
Sully, Jack 95-103
Sundance Kid (The) 30
Swearengen, Al 17-26, 53-54
Sweeney, Tom 82
Taylor, Joseph 85-86
Ticknor, Harry 29
Todd, John B.S. 1
Towle, Frank 32, 34
Towles, Kemsley 118
Tubbs, Warren 90-91
Utter, Charlie 46-47, 54-55, 133
Varnes, John 43
Voorhees, Luke 35, 78
Waite, Harry 61
Walker, Ted 94
Ward, Charlie 86
Wheeler 11
Wheeler, Edward 137
Wind Cave 108
Wintermute, Peter 5
Worth, Howard 61
Worthington, D.B. 108
Yankton 1-10, 15, 21, 39, 42-45, 49-50, 66, 106-107, 117
Yellow Doll 56
Young, Sam 41
Zimmerman, John 34